CHRISTMAS SONGS
MADE IN
AMERICA

Favorite Holiday Melodies and the
Stories of Their Origins

CHRISTMAS SONGS
MADE IN
AMERICA

Favorite Holiday Melodies and the
Stories of Their Origins

ALBERT J. MENENDEZ
& SHIRLEY C. MENENDEZ

Cumberland House
Nashville, Tennessee

Published by Cumberland House Publishing, Inc.
431 Harding Industrial Drive, Nashville, TN 37211

Book design by Karen Phillips

Library of Congress Cataloging-in-Publication Data

Menendez, Albert J.
    Christmas songs made in America : favorite holiday melodies and the stories of their origin / Albert J. Menendez & Shirley C. Menendez.
        p. cm.
    Includes bibliographical references and index.
    ISBN 1-581-82046-1 (hc. : alk. paper)
        1. Carols, English—United States—History and criticism. 2. Popular music—United States—History and criticism. 3. Christmas music—History and criticism. I. Title. II. Menendez, Shirley, 1937—

ML2881.U6 M46 1999
782.42'1723'0973 21--dc21

                                                                99-046610

Printed in the United States of America
1 2 3 4 5 6 7 8 - 03 02 01 00 99

For Barbara, Dorothy, Gladys, Mary, and Nancy
Thanks for the many wonderful
Christmases we have shared.

CONTENTS

INTRODUCTION

For many of us Christmas really isn't Christmas until the first songs of the season are heard. Our American celebration of Christmas is intimately linked to familiar and beloved sounds and tunes that retain their popularity by being heard and sung year after year. They are cherished friends whose annual visit is anticipated each Christmas season.

Readers might be familiar with different phrases in some of the songs in this book, since lyrics may have changed over the years. We have endeavored to include what we believe are the standard or most common versions.

Many of the great Christmas songs have a vitality and universality of appeal, such that the season would be incomplete without them. For *Christmas Songs Made in America*, we have selected some of the most hallowed and familiar Yuletide songs from many idioms—popular, folk, rock, sacred, and country. We tell the history behind these songs—the circumstances of their composition, anecdotes from those who composed or recorded them, and some reasons for their enduring popularity. It is hoped that these stories will add to your enjoyment when you hear the songs or sing them with family and friends.

All the songs selected herein were written by Americans and thus constitute a uniquely American contribution to the festive season. This is not meant, however, to be parochial by any means. It is probable that the most popular of all songs is the carol "Silent Night," bequeathed to all the world by two Austrians. In fact, Scripps Howard News Service and Ohio

University conducted a 1998 national survey of American adults concerning the role of Christmas in American life, and "Silent Night" was the clear winner among the carols named as favorites. Five of the top ten favorite carols were of American origin, including "Jingle Bells," "White Christmas," "The Little Drummer Boy," "Rudolph the Red-Nosed Reindeer," and "Away in a Manger." The popularity of Christmas music remains high, as evidenced by the fact that 76 percent of those surveyed named a favorite Christmas song compared, for example, to the 59 percent who said they planned to attend a Christmas worship service.

While there are countless songs from England, France, Germany, Italy, and dozens of other lands that are an indispensable part of our Christmas musical repertories, very little has been written about the American-born-and-bred songs of Christmas. Let the following stories enrich your celebration of this most joyous of holidays.

CHRISTMAS SONGS
MADE IN
AMERICA

Favorite Holiday Melodies and the
Stories of Their Origins

CELEBRATING
THE SEASON

Christmas is a season as much as it is a day or a series of days at the beginning of the Winter Solstice. The selection of December 25 by the fourth-century Church was as much a political decision to counter already established and popular "pagan" (or "pre-Christian") festivities as it was a spiritual move based on historical certitude.

But the calendar has a way of creating moods and embellishing the setting, as does the weather. Since Christmas is largely a western hemisphere and north-of-the-equator phenomenon in cultural terms, it is no surprise that Christmas memories and customs are shaped by and rooted in a time of year that is cold, dark, and often snowy.

While millions of Christmas lovers have never seen snowdrifts, icicles on the branches, or snowmen on the lawn, they seem to enjoy holiday songs that celebrate the seasonal surroundings as much as those who *do* live in cold climes.

The songs in this section delight in the cold weather that, in the minds of the composers at least, characterizes a "real" Christmas. Come to think of it, there are a lot more Christmas cards with Currier and Ives snow scenes than there are of Southern California malls or Key West marinas. Like it or not, we are stuck with the image of Christmas as a time when snowflakes are falling and fireplace logs are burning.

"CAROLING, CAROLING"

This lovely carol reflects the joy of singing and the centrality of music in the annual celebrations surrounding the Christmas season. "Caroling, Caroling" is memorable because of its upbeat melody, its repetition of the words "ding, dong, ding, dong, Christmas bells are ringing," and its overall joyful mood. Such phrases as "gladsome tidings now we bring" and "joyous voices sweet and clear" that will "sing the sad of heart to cheer" make this a song to cherish each Christmas.

Its appearance in 1954 came at the end of the short but vibrant musical career of Alfred Burt, a still relatively unknown American composer. Burt was born on April 22, 1920, in the small, scenic town of Marquette, Michigan, in the state's rugged Upper Peninsula region. Marquette was, and is, a town of remarkable diversity, with large numbers of citizens claiming Finnish, French, German, and Swedish ancestry.

Burt's father, Bates Gilbert Burt, was the rector of Saint Paul's Episcopal Church, and Alfred was born in the rectory. Two years later the family moved to All Saints' Episcopal

Church in Pontiac, Michigan, where Alfred soon discovered his musical talents. His life was centered on the Church and on music. He received a cornet at age ten "as a bribe to enter the local hospital for an appendectomy," his wife Anne remembers. He won many awards for his playing, and his earliest compositions were trumpet and horn fanfares for Christmas and Easter.

Burt's father was a self-taught musician, who enjoyed composing Christmas carols as cards for his friends and parishioners. Burt's widow Anne wrote, "Through Father Burt's creative talents, the tradition began of sending an original carol as a Christmas card to friends and parishioners. He wrote both the music of the season and the words of faith from 1922 to 1941. The carols were as natural an expression of the Burt Christmas as the spicy tree in the rectory or Mother Burt's famous plum pudding."

After graduating from the University of Michigan School of Music in 1942, Burt served in the Army Air Force Band. He wrote the music to two of his father's Christmas carols, "Jesu Parvule" and "What Are the Signs," as well as an anthem, "They That Wait Upon the Lord."

Burt married his high school sweetheart, Anne Shortt, in 1945. He played in bands, taught music in New York, and then joined the Alvino Rey Orchestra in 1949, which took the family to California. Burt continued his father's tradition of composing an original Christmas carol for friends and sending them as cards. He used words written by his father, but after his father's death in 1948, Burt's friend, organist Wihla Hutson, wrote the words for his annual card list, which had grown to 450 names by 1951. Hutson and Burt collaborated on a lullaby, "Sleep, Baby Mine," and on such tender songs as "This is Christmas" and "Some Children See Him."

Life was happy and fulfilling for the young couple. Their daughter Diane was born in 1950, but just a few years later, in 1953, a medical diagnosis brought the tragic news that Burt had terminal cancer.

He faced the end courageously, supported by a wide circle of family and friends. Columbia Records announced plans to record all of Alfred Burt's Christmas carols, believing that collectively they represented a major contribution to the musical traditions of Christmas. Wihla Hutson wrote four carols for the album, including "Caroling, Caroling." The King Sisters, Buddy Cole, and Jimmy Joyce premiered these last songs in a Hollywood church. The stirring and triumphant "O, Hearken Ye" became the Burt family's 1953 Christmas card.

Just four days before his death in February 1954, Burt completed his final carol, "The Star Carol," making a last-minute change to reflect his high standards of professionalism. He died at the age of thirty-three, just an hour before the signed contract from Columbia Records arrived by special messenger.

Burt's widow Anne, who still lives in Northridge, California, remembers the 1954 Christmas card: "The red, green, and white card was the loveliest card we had ever sent. It was signed simply, 'Anne and Diane.' Inside I tucked a note telling of the end of our tradition with Al's death and the release of the music for all to enjoy. Our legacy of love was our gift of music to the world that Christmas. Since then the music of Alfred S. Burt has taken its place in the heritage of American music."

Anne has devoted her life to the preservation of her husband's memory as a unique composer of Christmas music. Their daughter, Diane, is an actress, singer, and musical director whose Caroling Company sings Burt's carols and other familiar songs.

Burt's complete Christmas collection was published by Columbia and called *The Christmas Mood*. It is still available on CD. Another CD, *This Is Christmas*, features "The Voices of Jimmy Joyce," a sixteen-voice a cappella choir. Many of Burt's songs have a prayerful, spiritual mood and a haunting quality that evokes medieval England, while the others, including "Caroling, Caroling," suggest the modern American preoccupation with family and the search for joy and happiness that envelop Christmastide.

Musicologist William Studwell believes that "the Alfred Burt Carols comprise one of the most significant bodies of holiday songs ever produced by one artist."

"Caroling, Caroling"

Caroling, caroling, now we go;
Christmas bells are ringing!
Caroling, caroling, thru the snow;
Christmas bells are ringing!
Joyous voices sweet and clear,
Sing the sad of heart to cheer,

Ding, dong, ding, dong,
Christmas bells are ringing!

Caroling, caroling, thru the town;
Christmas bells are ringing!
Caroling, caroling, up and down;
Christmas bells are ringing!
Mark ye well the song we sing,
Gladsome tidings now we bring,
Ding, dong, ding, dong,
Christmas bells are ringing!

Caroling, caroling, near and far;
Christmas bells are ringing!
Following, following, yonder star;
Christmas bells are ringing!
Sing we all this happy morn,
"Lo, the King of heav'n is born!"
Ding, dong, ding, dong,
Christmas bells are ringing!

"A HOLLY JOLLY CHRISTMAS"

A certain playful naughtiness can be discerned in this effervescent carol by Johnny Marks, a composer who seemed to have a knack for writing cheerful and affable songs for the season. Marks was born in Mount Vernon, New York, in 1909, attended Columbia University, and studied music in Paris. He worked most of his life as a radio producer, and he produced shows overseas for the army during World War II. He died in New York City in 1985.

"A Holly Jolly Christmas" is first and foremost a wish for Christmas happiness, with the references to "a cup of cheer" and kissing someone special under the mistletoe. There's no real "message" here, just a wish from composer to listener to lighten up and enjoy the holiday, even when it doesn't snow.

The great folk song maestro, Burl Ives, sang this song in the 1964 television special *Rudolph the Red-Nosed Reindeer*. His interpretation seemed right on the mark.

"A Holly Jolly Christmas"

Have a holly jolly Christmas,
It's the best time of the year.
I don't know if there'll be snow
But have a cup of cheer.

Have a holly jolly Christmas,
And when you walk down the street
Say hello to friends you know
And everyone you meet.

Oh, ho, the mistletoe
Hung where you can see.
Somebody waits for you,
Kiss her once for me.

Have a holly jolly Christmas,
And in case you didn't hear,
Oh, by golly, have a holly,
Jolly Christmas this year.

"IT'S BEGINNING TO LOOK LIKE CHRISTMAS"

This 1951 carol conveys a mood of pleasantry and of seasonal celebration. The music is lively, hummable, and easily recognizable, having been featured on many musical programs for almost half a century. It invariably appears on radio and in public places as the Christmas shopping season begins (earlier every year, it seems).

Some of the words clearly belong to a simpler time and place. The song mentions, for example, five-and-ten-cent stores, Hopalong Cassidy books and pistols for boys, and talking dolls for girls, as well as a tree in the "Grand Hotel."

Humorous touches have stood the test of time. "Mom and Dad can hardly wait for school to start again" is a universal sentiment. But all is well in this crazy world, especially since "the carol that you sing right within your heart" is the linchpin of all Christmas celebrations.

The great Meredith Wilson gave us this song. He was a veritable factory of musical talent. Born in Mason City, Iowa, in 1902, Wilson studied music at what is now the Julliard School in New York. He played the flute in John Philip Sousa's band and was flutist in the New York Philharmonic Symphony. After moving to Hollywood, Wilson became music director for the Burns and Allen radio show, composed scores for *The Great Dictator* and *The Little Foxes*, and served as a major in the U.S. Army during World War II.

Wilson later had his own television show during the medium's infancy, in 1949, and was the music director of radio's last variety program, *The Big Show*, featuring the awesome Tallulah Bankhead.

Wilson's 1950 composition, "May the Good Lord Bless and Keep You," was recorded by Frankie Laine and became the most-requested song by American troops during the Korean War.

His claim to musical fame rests largely on the success of *The Music Man* in 1957, his first stage musical, for which he wrote the book, lyrics, and music from recollections of his Iowa boyhood. Starring Robert Preston and Barbara Cook, this rousing small-town saga opened on Broadway on December 19, 1957, and completed 1,375 performances. Wilson won the Tony Award and Grammies for such delightful tunes as "Till There Was You" and "Seventy-Six Trombones."

He then wrote *The Unsinkable Molly Brown*, which opened in 1960 and ran for 532 performances. Wilson returned to the Christmas theme in 1963 when his musical, *Here's Love*, opened on Broadway and ran for 334 performances. *Here's Love* was a stage version of *Miracle on 34th Street*, the popular 1947 book and film created by Valentine Davies. Wilson used "It's Beginning to Look Like Christmas" in his play, along with a charming song titled "Pine Cones and Holly Berries." Perry Como and the Fontaine Sisters recorded "It's Beginning to Look Like Christmas" in 1951, and it reached the Top Twenty on the pop charts.

"It's Beginning to Look Like Christmas"

*It's beginning to look a lot like Christmas
Ev'rywhere you go;
Take a look in the five-and-ten, glistening once again,
With candy canes and silver lanes aglow.*

*It's beginning to look a lot like Christmas;
Toys in ev'ry store,
But the prettiest sight to see is the holly that will be
On your own front door.*

*A pair of Hopalong boots and a pistol that shoots
Is the wish of Barney and Ben,
Dolls that will talk and will go for a walk
Is the hope of Janice and Jen;
And Mom and Dad can hardly wait for school to start again.*

*It's beginning to look a lot like Christmas
Ev'rywhere you go;
There's a tree in the Grand Hotel, one in the park as well,
The sturdy kind that doesn't mind the snow.*

*It's beginning to look a lot like Christmas;
Soon the bells will start,
And the thing that will make them ring is the carol that you sing
Right within your heart.*

"JINGLE BELLS"

This holiday-season classic has had one of the longest runs in American musical history. Written in 1857, "Jingle Bells" is still enormously popular today. It is included in almost every Christmas musical program, even with lyrics that do not mention the nativity or the Christmas holiday itself.

Even though the lyrics to "Jingle Bells" seem dated with references to "open sleighs" and "bells on bobtail," its popularity has spread far beyond rural New England, where people would immediately identify with it. The romance of snow, the clear references to young people dating and having a good time, and the popularity of horses gave the song a universal appeal that transcended time.

It is probable that this is the earliest secular Christmas song written in the United States, though two other songs, "Up on the Housetop" and "Jolly Old Saint Nicholas," date from the same period.

Glenn Miller's 1941 version of "Jingle Bells" was popular. During World War II, when Americans needed reassurance, Bing Crosby and the Andrews Sisters recorded this song for Decca. More than a million copies of the record were sold in 1943 alone.

James S. Pierpont, of Boston, wrote both the lyrics and the music for this bouncy, lively song for his father's Sunday school class on Thanksgiving 1857. This New England-oriented holiday was then more popular than Christmas in much of the country. One of Pierpont's friends promptly called it "a merry little jingle," and its snappy tune soon caught on wherever it was presented. Originally called "The One Horse Open Sleigh," the song was so popular that Sunday schoolers were asked to repeat it for Christmas.

Pierpont was a modest man and did not really think that he had written a song that would endure. He did not even take much credit for it until the *Salem Evening News* presented a feature article on it in 1864. Recent evidence, however, suggests that he might have borrowed lines from a song by Stephen Foster or from another song popularized by Christy's Minstrels.

Pierpont came from a prominent New England Unitarian family that held abolitionist views on slavery, although he supported the Confederate cause in the Civil War. He even moved to the South and wrote two songs extolling the Lost Cause: "We Conquer or Die" and "Strike for the South."

Pierpont, uncle to the millionaire financier John Pierpont Morgan, was adventurous as a lad, running off to sea and eventually ending up in California during the gold rush. By 1852 he had become the organist for a Savannah, Georgia, church pastored by his brother.

Pierpont died in Winter Haven, Florida, in 1893 and is buried in Savannah at Laurel Grove Cemetery. A marker honoring him was unveiled in June 1985 in Troup Square, one of Savannah's many beautiful parks.

Long popular with both children and adults, Pierpont's "Jingle Bells" continues to find new audiences. Dan Fox, in his *Classic Christmas Carols and Songs,* calls it "arguably the best-known Christmas song in the world."

"Jingle Bells"

Dashing through the snow,
In a one horse open sleigh,
O'er the fields we go
Laughing all the way.
Bells on bobtail ring,
Making spirits bright,
What fun it is to ride and sing
A sleighing song to night!

(Refrain:)
Oh! Jingle bells, jingle bells,
Jingle all the way.
Oh what fun it is to ride
In a one horse open sleigh!

Jingle bells, jingle bells,
Jingle all the way.
Oh what fun it is to ride
In a one horse open sleigh!

A day or two ago
I thought I'd take a ride;
And soon Miss Fannie Bright
Was seated by my side.
The horse was lean and lank,

Misfortune seemed his lot,
He got into a drifted bank
And we, we got upsot!

(Refrain)

Now the ground is white
Go it while you're young.
Take the girls tonight
And sing this sleighing song.
Just get a bobtail bay,
Two forty for his speed,
Then hitch him to an open
Sleigh and crack!
You'll take the lead!

(Refrain)

"A MARSHMALLOW WORLD"

Winter lovers (and there are many, believe it or not) are attracted to this light and frothy song that mixes the metaphors of wintry weather and sweet confections.

A rather dreamy vision is conveyed, and there is a sense of being suspended in time, enveloped in a friendly, snowy world that is compared to whipped cream, sugar dates, and marshmallows. "It's a yum-yummy world made of sweethearts," says the opening of the fourth verse.

Admittedly, this may be too saccharine a song for some

listeners, and its old-fashioned language may be a bit too "fluffy." But as a kind of period piece or just background music, it works well enough.

Carl Sigman, a Brooklyn native, composed "A Marshmallow World" in 1949. Sigman had attended New York University Law School and won the Bronze Star during World War II as a member of the 82nd Airborne Division. Turning to music after the war, Sigman scored the Broadway musical *Angel in the Wings* in 1947. As a lyricist, Sigman also wrote "Enjoy Yourself," "My Heart Cries for You," "Arrivederci, Roma," and "Pennsylvania 6-5000." His collaborator was Peter DeRose.

"A Marshmallow World" has been recorded by Vic Damone, Arthur Godfrey, Vaughn Monroe, and the Four Knights, among others.

"A Marshmallow World"

It's a marshmallow world in the winter,
When the snow comes to cover the ground.
It's time for play, it's a whipped cream day.
I wait for it the whole year round.

These marshmallow clouds being friendly
In the arms of the evergreen trees,
And the sun is red, like a pumpkin head,
It's shining so your nose won't freeze.

The world is your snowball, see how it grows.
That's how it goes, wherever it snows.

The world is your snowball just for a song,
Get out and roll it along.

It's a yum-yummy world made for sweethearts,
Take a walk with your favorite girl.
It's a sugar date, what if spring is late.
In winter, it's a marshmallow world.

"SLEIGH RIDE"

Written and composed just after World War II, "Sleigh Ride" easily fits into the category of light-hearted, celebratory songs contributing to the musical era of good feelings that prevailed in those early postwar years (despite the Cold War, Korea, and threats of nuclear destruction).

The music was composed by the highly talented Leroy Anderson, born to a Swedish-American family in Cambridge, Massachusetts, in 1908. Anderson studied at the New England Conservatory of Music and at Harvard, became an organist and choirmaster, and was orchestrator and arranger with the Boston Pops Orchestra and its celebrated conductor Arthur Fiedler.

After serving in the army from 1942 to 1946, Anderson returned to the world of music and began to create his own compositions, including "Fiddle Faddle," "The Syncopated Clock," and "Blue Tango." In 1948 he composed "Sleigh Ride" as a purely orchestral or instrumental work, with his imaginative recreations of the sounds of a genuine sleigh.

Two years later lyricist Mitchell Parish added some magic of his own. His words brought the music to life with their

images of a snowy wonderland and two lovebirds snuggling together in an idyllic rural landscape. References to Farmer Gray's home, to Currier and Ives prints, and to homey things such as coffee and pumpkin pie make it appropriate to the season, even if Christmastime itself is never mentioned.

Parish was born in 1900 in Shreveport, Louisiana, and grew up in New York City. After abandoning a planned career in medicine, he applied his talents to songwriting and is remembered today for such classics as "It's Wonderful," "Stars Fell on Alabama," and "All I Need Is You."

Parish died in 1993, Anderson in 1975.

"Sleigh Ride"

Just hear those sleigh bells jingling,
Ring ting tingling too.
Come on, it's lovely weather
For a sleigh ride together with you.

Outside the snow is falling,
And friends are calling "Yoo Hoo."
Come on, it's lovely weather
For a sleigh ride together with you.

Giddy-yap, giddy-yap, giddy-yap
Let's go.
Let's look at the snow.
We're riding in a wonderland of snow.

Giddy-yap, giddy-yap, giddy-yap it's grand
Just holding your hand.
We're gliding along with a song
Of a wintry fairy land.

Our cheeks are nice and rosy
And comfy cozy are we.
We're snuggled up together like two
Birds of a feather would be.

Let's take that road before us
And sing a chorus or two.

Come on, it's lovely weather
For a sleigh ride together with you.

There's a birthday party at the home of Farmer Gray.
It'll be the perfect ending of a perfect day.
We'll be singing the songs we love to sing without a single stop
At the fireplace while we watch the chestnuts pop
Pop! Pop! Pop!

There's a happy feeling nothing in the world can buy
When they pass around the chocolate and the pumpkin pie.
It'll nearly be like a picture print by Currier and Ives.
These wonderful things are the things
We remember all through our lives.

(Repeat first stanza)

"WINTER WONDERLAND"

Another celebration of the delights of winter, "Winter Wonderland" conveys the joys of the holiday season as a young couple discovers their love for each other. The scenes described are fairly commonplace: sleigh bells ringing, snow glistening, a snowman being built, and dreaming of future happiness by a warm fire. All those visuals are appealing, even to those whose experiences may be vicarious (if they grew up in Southern California or Key West, for example).

The lyrics to this enjoyable and familiar song were written in 1934 by Richard Smith. The music was composed by Felix

Bernard, a one-time vaudeville performer and tap dancer. Bernard, born in Brooklyn in 1897, came from a musical family. His father was a professional violinist, and Felix became a composer and pianist. Bernard wrote "Dardanella" in 1919. A recording of it became the first record of dance hall music to sell over a million copies.

Guy Lombardo and his Royal Canadians were the first to record "Winter Wonderland," and their version was number two on the Hit Parade in 1934. The Andrews Sisters arranged "Winter Wonderland" with their special style and made it a big hit in 1950. Perry Como, whose status as a Christmas songster rivaled Bing Crosby's, also hit the Top Ten with his crooner's version.

Unfortunately, neither Smith nor Bernard lived to see their song's considerable popularity. Smith died at age thirty-four the year after he wrote the words, and Bernard passed away in 1944.

"Winter Wonderland"

Sleigh bells ring, are you list'nin?
In the lane snow is glist'nin,
A beautiful sight, we're happy tonight,
Walkin' in a winter wonderland!

Gone away is the blue bird,
Here to stay is a new bird,
He sings a love song as we go along,
Walkin' in a winter wonderland!

In the meadow we can build a snowman,
Then pretend that he is Parson Brown;
He'll say, "Are you married?" We'll say, "No, man!
But you can do the job when you're in town!"

Later on we'll conspire
As we dream by the fire,
To face unafraid the plans that we made,
Walkin' in a winter wonderland!

Sleigh bells ring, are you list'nin?
In the lane snow is glist'nin,
A beautiful sight, we're happy tonight,
Walkin' in a winter wonderland!

Gone away is the blue bird,
Here to stay is a new bird,
He's singing a song as we go along,
Walkin' in a winter wonderland!

In the meadow we can build a snowman,
And pretend that he's a circus clown;
We'll have lots of fun with Mister Snowman,
Until the other kiddies knock 'im down!

When it snows, ain't it thrillin',
Tho' your nose gets a chillin'?
We'll frolic and play the Eskimo way,
Walkin' in a winter wonderland!

II

HEARTH AND HOME

Christmas means many things to many people. But it is always a time for families to get together and for friends to renew their friendships. Clearly, most Americans see Christmas as the preeminent family festival, as evidenced through the years by various polls.

President Harry Truman told his fellow Americans on his last Christmas in the White House, "Christmas is the great home festival. It is the day in all the year which turns our thoughts toward home."

Echoing those sentiments three decades later, President Ronald Reagan, in his first White House Christmas message, told his listeners, "At Christmastime every home takes on a special beauty, a special warmth."

The songs highlighted in this section reflect the many moods of Christmas at home.

"BLUE CHRISTMAS"

Ernest Tubb's Decca recording of "Blue Christmas" was a solid seller in 1949, reaching number one on the charts. It continued at number two in 1950 and 1951. This poignant lament for a lost love contrasted the traditional Christmas colors of red and green, with blue as a symbol of heartache and loss.

It was also recorded in 1949 by Russ Morgan and Hugo Winterhalter. In 1950 Billy Eckstine added his own inimitable touch to the song, which was written by Billy Hayes and Jay Johnson.

But it was the great Ernest Tubb, "the Texas Troubadour," who first made this a hit in the years of readjustment and change in American life following World War II.

Tubb was born in 1914 in the tiny farm town of Crisp in Ellis County, Texas. Tubb has been called "the ultimate honky-tonk vocalist and stylist." Signing a record deal with Decca, Tubb recorded "Walking the Floor Over You" and a number of other hits. Joining the *Grand Ole Opry* as a regular in January 1943, he soon starred in the film *Hollywood Barn Dance* and then opened his famous Ernest Tubb Record Shop in Nashville, showing that he had entrepreneurial as well as musical skills. His duet with Red Foley, "Goodnight Irene," was popular. He was inducted into the Country Music Hall of Fame in 1965. His musical career continued for two decades, though emphysema slowed him down and eventually caused his death in 1984.

Elvis Presley made another popular recording of "Blue Christmas." He loved the Christmas holidays and delighted in giving lavish gifts to friends, colleagues, and loved ones.

Presley was fond of the music and exhibited a childlike awe of the season.

In 1968, during his comeback period, Elvis recorded a Christmas special, telecast on December 3. His manager, Colonel Tom Parker, wanted Elvis to wear a tuxedo. But his producer, Steve Bender, thought Elvis's legion of fans would find his appearance stuffy and inappropriate. So did Elvis, who chose a casual look while he sang a medley of Christmas and non-Christmas songs, closing with "If I Can Dream."

During the program Elvis looked straight at the audience and announced, "I'd like to do my favorite Christmas song." He proceeded to sing "Blue Christmas" in a soulful manner, low and throaty, while strumming his guitar.

Elvis recorded a Christmas album early in his career, when his 1957 "Elvis's Christmas" for RCA was number one on the charts. Years later he recorded "If Every Day Was Like Christmas." Presley's 1964 single of "Blue Christmas" is the sixth most popular Christmas recording of all time, according to researcher Craig Pattillo. Other Christmas records include "Memories of Christmas" and "Elvis Sings the Wonderful World of Christmas."

"Blue Christmas"

I'll have a blue Christmas without you;
I'll be so blue thinkin' about you.
Decorations of red on a green Christmas tree
Won't mean a thing if you're not here with me.

I'll have a blue Christmas, that's certain;
And when that blue heartache starts hurtin',
You'll be doin' all right with your Christmas of white,
But I'll have a blue, blue Christmas.

"THE CHRISTMAS SONG (CHESTNUTS ROASTING ON AN OPEN FIRE)"

"Chestnuts roasting on an open fire, Jack Frost nipping at your nose." What other song's opening verse conjures up a more contented feeling of home and hearth? This 1946 ballad composed by lyricist Robert Wells and singer-songwriter Mel Torme is a good example of the Christmas-in-July syndrome. This slow-tempo, wintry-feeling song first saw the light of day on a broiling July afternoon.

In his autobiography, *It Wasn't All Velvet*, Torme remembered driving to Wells's Toluca Lake home "one excessively hot afternoon as the San Fernando Valley blistered in the July sun." Opening the front door and walking to the piano, Torme spotted a writing pad on the music board with the four opening lines of a Christmas ditty. When Wells appeared, dressed in tennis shorts and a white T-shirt, he said it was so hot that he "wrote something to cool myself off, and all I could think of was Christmas and cold weather."

Torme was captivated. He wrote, "I took another look at his handiwork and thought this just might make a song. We sat down together at the piano, and, improbable though it may sound, 'The Christmas Song' was completed about forty-five minutes later."

Wells added that his memories of chestnuts sold by vendors on the streets of New York contributed to his vision of the holiday. His inspiration was seeing a bag of chestnuts that his mother was planning to use for the stuffing for his birthday turkey dinner.

The duo, who had been working together on the title song for *Abie's Irish Rose* and for *Magic Town*, starring James Stewart and Jane Wyman, promptly drove into Hollywood and played it for several friends, including Nat King Cole.

Cole and his wife Maria, as well as Capitol record executives, saw a hit in the making. Cole recorded the song with strings and a studio orchestra, and the public loved it. By November 30, 1946, it rose to number three on the charts and remained near the top for seven weeks. Cole's biographer, James Haskins, wrote that Cole's version of "The Christmas Song" "set a new fashion in standard Christmas tunes, selling so well that other popular singers rushed to record it. But it was forever after associated primarily with Cole. He loved the song and always regarded it as one of his favorites."

During his illustrious career Cole also recorded some now-forgotten Christmas songs, such as "The Little Boy That Santa Claus Forgot" and "Take Me Back to Toyland."

Of all the songs he wrote, Torme will be forever remembered for "The Christmas Song." When he was married in a judge's chambers on Saint Thomas in 1984, the judge played

"The Christmas Song" just before the ceremony. Torme also wrote "Christmas Was Made for Children," which was admired by Bing Crosby but is not often heard today.

"The Christmas Song (Chestnuts Roasting on an Open Fire)"

Chestnuts roasting on an open fire,
Jack Frost nipping at your nose,
Yuletide carols being sung by a choir
And folks dressed up like Eskimos.

Everybody knows a turkey and some mistletoe
Help to make the season bright.
Tiny tots with their eyes all aglow
Will find it hard to sleep tonight.

They know that Santa's on his way;
He's loaded lots of toys and goodies on his sleigh.
And every mother's child is gonna spy
To see if reindeer really know how to fly.

And so, I'm offering this simple phrase
To kids from one to ninety-two.
Altho' it's been said many times, many ways;
"Merry Christmas to you."

"I'LL BE HOME FOR CHRISTMAS"

"I'll Be Home for Christmas" took the country by storm in the war year of 1943. Bing Crosby's smooth and melodic version was the top-selling Christmas song that year. More than a million copies have been sold over the years.

The words alone made this a sentimental tearjerker as well as a tender song of longing for peace, security, and the joys of home—all things that were threatened by the terrible conflict that then engulfed the world.

The singer—possibly a soldier, and certainly someone separated from the people and places that he or she loved—sets the tone from the first line, "I'm dreaming tonight of a place I love, even more than I usually do." As Christmas approaches, the sense of loss becomes even more acute. A plaintive appeal for "snow and mistletoe and presents on the tree" tugs at the heartstrings. The last line, "if only in my dreams," completes the dreamlike quality, the sense of longing for what cannot be. It has always been a heartrending song for those whose loved ones never came home for Christmas.

As a wartime song of faith and hope, it ranks with "God Bless America" and "There'll Always Be an England," two songs of the allied nations that gave a much-needed dose of perspective to a struggle that touched the lives of everyone.

The lyricist was Kim Gannon, a Brooklyner, and the music was written by Walter Kent, a Manhattan-born composer. Kent also wrote the music for "The White Cliffs of Dover," another wartime song popular on both sides of the Atlantic.

Perry Como and Joni James also recorded popular versions of this song.

"I'll Be Home for Christmas"

I'm dreaming tonight of a place I love,
Even more than I usually do.
And although I know it's a long road back,
I promise you

I'll be home for Christmas,
You can count on me.

Please have snow and mistletoe
And presents on the tree.

Christmas Eve will find me
Where the love light gleams,
I'll be home for Christmas,
If only in my dreams.

"LET IT SNOW! LET IT SNOW! LET IT SNOW!"

This very melodic classic mixes romance with the weather to create a delightfully cozy song that has always appealed to couples and lovers. Who wouldn't want to be more or less stranded in a snowstorm with one's beloved?

The lyrics have a certain pre-1960s innocence about them, referring to goodnight kisses, parting for the night, and popping corn. Delicacy and charm characterize the four brief stanzas.

Musician Jule Styne and lyricist Sammy Cahn collaborated on this popular song, as they did for many others. Styne was born in London on New Year's Eve 1905 but raised in Chicago. A child prodigy on the piano, he elected to join the popular music circuit and organized his own dance band in 1931. After some time on the Chicago hotel and club circuit, Styne went to Hollywood and became the vocal coach for Alice Faye, Linda Darnell, and Shirley Temple.

Styne linked up with the New York City-born Cahn in 1942, and three years later they wrote "Let It Snow." This wintry delight was not written during a blizzard, though, but on a hot July day in Los Angeles. Styne and Cahn were finishing some business with their publisher Edwin H. Morris, and Cahn suggested they go to the beach for a swim. But the workaholic Styne suggested they cool off by writing a song with a winter theme. So what emerged was this affable and upbeat tune.

Vaughn Monroe helped to popularize the song, and his recording was the number-one Christmas song of 1945. The Ohio-born Monroe was a popular singer during the Big Band era. His first hit was "Racing With the Moon" in 1941, followed by "Ballerina" and "Ghost Riders in the Sky," a million-copy seller in 1949. Though trained at the New England Conservatory of Music, Monroe distinguished himself in the rhythm and blues field. He also appeared in a number of Western films, singing "Red Roses for a Blue Lady" in the 1950 flick *Singing Guns*. Later in life he opened a Massachusetts restaurant. He died in Stuart, Florida, in 1973 at the age of sixty-one.

Cahn, who died in 1992, wrote the words to "Love and Marriage," for which he won an Emmy, "High Hopes," "All the Way," and "Call Me Irresponsible." Styne, who passed away in 1994, wrote the complete score for *Bells Are Ringing, Gypsy, Funny Girl*, and *Subways Are for Sleeping*.

They collaborated on the 1947 Broadway hit, *High Button Shoes*, and won an Academy Award for the 1954 hit, *Three Coins in the Fountain*.

"Let It Snow! Let It Snow! Let It Snow!"

Oh the weather outside is frightful,
But the fire is so delightful,
And since we've no place to go,
Let it snow! Let it snow! Let it snow!

It doesn't show signs of stopping
And I brought some corn for popping,
The lights are turned way down low,
Let it snow! Let it snow! Let it snow!

When we finally kiss goodnight,
How I'll hate going out in the storm!
But if you'll really hold me tight,
All the way home I'll be warm.

The fire is slowly dying
And my dear we're still goodbyeing,
But as long as you love me so,
Let it snow! Let it snow! Let it snow!

"PRETTY PAPER"

Willie Nelson's unusual Christmas song expresses his well-known compassion for the downtrodden and disadvantaged. From the perspective of a poor, homeless man observing the hustle and bustle and indifference of prosperous Christmas shoppers, it is a bit of a downer—but wholly, and sadly, appropriate to modern-day life in America.

The first and last stanzas are conventional tributes to the beautiful paper and ribbons used for wrapping gifts to loved ones. Messages are written with pretty pencils. But the second stanza introduces a homeless man who "sits alone on the sidewalk," hoping that he will not be ignored by busy shoppers. In the third stanza, we find that people are much too busy to notice or assist him, and his tears form a counterpoint to their laughter.

Nelson's own version is beautifully moving but it was another Texan, Roy Orbison, who made this song a hit. Orbison was, like Nelson, something of a rebel and an individualist whose musical style is entirely distinctive. According to Ellis Amburn, Orbison's biographer, "Willie had sung the song to Roy in his hotel room, and Roy had loved the idea of having a seasonal hit." Recorded in London, it soon reached the Top Ten in England and number fifteen on the U.S. charts for 1963, which was an exceptional showing for a new Christmas number.

Orbison, whom Elvis Presley called "the greatest singer in the world," was born in Vernon, Texas, in 1936, the son of an oil field worker. He merged country and rockabilly into a blend of music that was uniquely his own. Some of his classic songs include "Oh Pretty Woman," "Crying," and "Only the Lonely." His tours were as popular in England as they were in the United States. Orbison's life was marked by tragedy when first wife Claudette was killed in a motorcycle accident in

1966. His two sons perished in a house fire two years later.

But his career continued to draw fans and respect. He sang duets with Emmylou Harris and k.d. lang and was inducted into the Rock and Roll Hall of Fame in 1987. Though his future looked promising, Orbison died of a heart attack the following year while visiting his mother in Madison, Tennessee.

Willie Nelson, born in 1933 in Abbott, Texas, is a versatile performer, songwriter, actor, and social conscience. Early in his career he wrote the song "Hello Walls," which became a number-one hit for Faron Young. Patsy Cline's recording of his "Crazy" became a major hit in 1963. In the 1970s he threw the first of his legendary Fourth of July picnics, had his first number-one hit with "Blue Eyes Crying in the Rain," and acted with Robert Redford in *The Electric Horseman*. He was also named Entertainer of the Year in 1979 by the Country Music Association.

Nelson's Farm Aid concerts have since the mid-1980s helped dramatize the plight of America's farmers. He has still managed to come up with a series of number-one hits including, "Forgiving You Was Easy," "Seven Spanish Angels," and "To All the Girls I've Loved Before" (with Julio Iglesias). In 1993 he was elected to the Country Music Hall of Fame.

"Pretty Paper"

Pretty paper, pretty ribbons of blue
Wrap your presents to your darling from you.

Pretty pencils to write I love you.
Pretty paper, pretty ribbons of blue.

Crowded streets, busy feet hustle by him.
Downtown shoppers. Christmas is nigh.
There he sits all alone on the sidewalk,
Hoping that you won't pass him by.

Should you stop? Better not, much too busy.
You'd better hurry. My, how time does fly.
And in the distance, the ringing of laughter.
And in the midst of the laughter he cries.

Pretty paper, pretty ribbons of blue
Wrap your presents to your darling from you.
Pretty pencils to write I love you.
Pretty paper, pretty ribbons of blue.

"THERE'S NO CHRISTMAS LIKE A HOME CHRISTMAS"

Carl Sigman, who wrote the words to "A Marshmallow World," collaborated with his composer partner Mike Addy to write this pleasant song. The words are catchy and convey a rather ordinary yearning to return to the safety and joy of family.

Sigman and Addy convey the expectation of welcome and home where "hearts" will be "humming at your homecoming." So, they say, everyone should follow the Christmas bells and return to the familiarity and comfort of home, "for that's the time of year all roads lead home." The last line is reminiscent of G. K. Chesterton's poem "The House of Christmas," where all of humanity is said to be "at home" at the stable in Bethlehem.

Sigman and Addy were completing a Christmas album when they discovered that they needed just one more song. So, in no time, this one emerged.

Perry Como and Englebert Humperdinck had modest successes with this now-familiar song.

"There's No Christmas Like a Home Christmas"

There is no Christmas like a home Christmas,
With your Dad and Mother, Sis and Brother there,
With their hearts humming at your homecoming,
And that merry Yuletide spirit in the air.

Christmas bells, Christmas bells, ringing loud and strong,
Follow them, follow them, you've been away too long.
There is no Christmas like a home Christmas,
For that's the time of year all roads lead home.

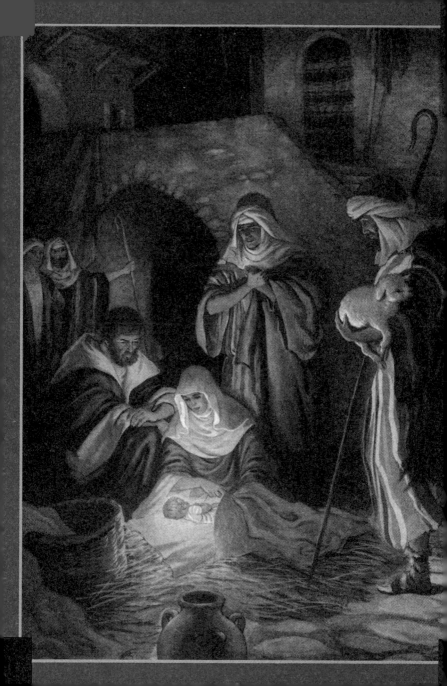

III

THE HOLY SEASON

In his *Stories of Christmas Carols*, Ernest K. Emurian suggested that Christmas music, like ancient Gaul, could be divided into three parts—hymns, carols, and songs. Christmas hymns, he said, were "religious poems written to be sung and addressed to or descriptive of one of the Persons of the Holy Trinity." Carols were not quite as formal or spiritual in content, format, and style. And songs were, well, more popular and secular in nature.

We're not sure if this definition is all that readily apparent today, since there is a considerable overlap between styles. But earlier generations tended to accept this division and to judge Christmas music accordingly.

Music historians do not agree on which song or hymn is America's first Christmas carol. Some have argued for the "Huron Carol" ("Jesus Is Born"), written in the early seventeenth century by a French missionary in a native American Indian language, though this more properly belongs to

Canada than to the United States. "Jesus Is Born" was preserved by Huron converts to Christianity after its author, Father Jean de Brebeuf, was put to death in 1649.

A good case can be made that "Shout the Glad Tidings" was the first American Christmas hymn. It was written by William Augustus Muhlenberg, rector of New York's historic Trinity Church, a Wall Street landmark, and the burial place of Alexander Hamilton. The Muhlenberg family contributed greatly to early American religious history, providing clergy to both the Lutheran and Episcopalian communities.

Muhlenberg based his short hymn on a verse from Isaiah. While it does not directly refer to the nativity, it was sung at Christmas in 1826 and soon became identified as a Christmas selection. President Andrew Jackson considered this his favorite Christmas song, according to Burl Ives and researchers who collaborated on Ives's recording "Christmas at the White House."

Most American churches that celebrate Christmas formerly used music written in Europe, often centuries before. But by the mid-nineteenth century, American composers began to offer their own creations to a realm of sacred music, and they still bring joy and hope to listeners as the twenty-first century dawns.

"AWAY IN A MANGER"

This familiar carol has long been popular, especially with children. Its tender, simple verses are so personal in nature that those who sing it or hum along to it feel transported back to Bethlehem.

It is an example of a lullaby, a kind of sub-category of poetry and of Christmas carol literature. It is meant to be sung to a baby or young child. Jesus is addressed as Lord, and he is depicted as sleeping on hay with "no crib for a bed." The third stanza suggests that the baby Jesus does not cry much, which may be wishful thinking or poetic fancy on the part of the author!

The fifth and sixth stanzas change character somewhat, addressing Jesus in heaven and pleading with Him to stay close to the petitioner and to bless all children.

The lullaby has been a rich part of religious poetry and of Christian folklore and music. Robert Herrick's "The Burning Babe" may be the most literate example of the form. A fifteenth-century carol from Chester, England, "Lully lully la" is an early example of the lullaby, as is the Czech carol "Jesus Dear, Sleep in Peace."

Many people will be surprised to learn that "Away in a Manger" is American in origin and was not written by Martin Luther in the sixteenth century. The musical scholars who prepared the *Companion to the Hymnal: A Handbook to the 1964 Methodist Hymnal* had this to say: "All that can be said confidently about the origin of this carol is that Martin Luther himself had nothing to do with it. The evidence suggests that it is wholly an American product. The original form probably originated among German Lutherans in Pennsylvania about 1885."

This is an example of how an inaccuracy can be compounded through the years. Anonymous verses entitled "Away in a Manger" appeared in 1885 in a book called *Little Children's Book for Schools and Family* published in Philadelphia by the

Evangelical Lutheran Church in North America. In 1887 "Away in a Manger" appeared again in James Ramsey Murray's *Dainty Songs for Little Lads and Lasses*, which called this "Luther's Cradle Hymn." Since the initials *JRM* appear in the upper right corner, Murray evidently wrote the music for this lullaby. Why he chose to perpetuate the ruse of Luther as the author of the lyrics is a mystery. Perhaps he wanted to capitalize on the Luther name since Luther was enormously popular in nineteenth-century America, and 1883 was the four hundredth anniversary of Luther's birth.

The myth was repeated until a brilliant work refuting it was written by Richard S. Hill in the "Music Library Association Notes" in December 1945. Through painstaking and exhaustive research, Hill concluded that there was no German original of "Away in a Manger" in Luther's voluminous writings, which had been published and translated for more than four centuries. None of Luther's many biographies had ever alluded to such a work, even though Luther wrote many carols, including the well-known "Von Himmel Hoch" (From Heaven on High I Come.")

There are many musical settings, all written by Americans. *The Hymnal Companion 1940* (Episcopal) noted, "By 1891 the carol was sweeping the country, largely due to Murray's repeated publication of his setting. During 1891 four new musical settings appeared, with three more in the following year." *The Episcopal Hymnal* uses an 1895 tune by William Kirkpatrick. Some other church hymnals prefer J. B. Herbert's 1891 version. Others prefer a tune written by Jonathan Spilman.

Even today, more than fifty years after its origins were definitively established, songbooks still refer to this as "Luther's Cradle Hymn."

"Away in a Manger"

Away in a manger,
No crib for a bed,
The little Lord Jesus
Laid down His sweet head.

The stars in the sky
Looked down where He lay,
The little Lord Jesus,
Asleep on the hay.

The cattle are lowing,
The Baby awakes,
But little Lord Jesus,
No crying He makes.

I love thee, Lord Jesus,
Look down from the sky,
And stay by my cradle
Till morning is nigh.

Be near me, Lord Jesus
I ask Thee to stay,
Close by me forever
And love me, I pray.

Bless all the dear children
In Thy tender care,
And take us to heaven
To live with Thee there.

"DO YOU HEAR WHAT I HEAR"

Here's a song that has a captivating quality that almost requires listeners to stop and meditate on the words. In this gentle retelling of the nativity, authors Noel Regney and Gloria Shayne use elements ("the night wind"), animals ("the little lamb") as well as a "shepherd boy," and "a mighty king" to convey the message that this child "will bring goodness and light to people everywhere."

The words are relatively simple but seem perfectly appropriate to a carol that builds its story little by little, like a ballad. Having one character ask a question to another, *e.g.*, "Do you see what I see?" "Do you hear what I hear?" and "Do you know what I know?" is a nice touch. The contrast between a mighty king who lives "in a warm palace" and a child who "shivers in the cold" paints a word picture that is gripping.

This beautiful song, which seems to fall somewhere between a carol and hymn, was written in 1962. William Studwell calls it "the only well-known American Christmas song since World War II with a clearly religious tone." It is both memorable and beautiful.

Anita Bryant, the Harry Simeone Chorale, Charlie Byrd, and Andy Williams all had strong sellers with this carol.

"Do You Hear What I Hear"

Said the night wind to the little lamb,
Do you see what I see?
Way up in the sky, little lamb,
Do you see what I see?
A star, a star, dancing in the night
With a tail as big as a kite,
With a tail as big as a kite.

Said the little lamb to the shepherd boy,
Do you hear what I hear?
Ringing thru the sky, shepherd boy,
Do you hear what I hear?
A song, a song, high above the tree
With a voice as big as the sea,
With a voice as big as the sea.

Said the shepherd boy to the mighty king,
Do you know what I know?
In your palace warm, mighty king,
Do you know what I know?
A Child, a Child, shivers in the cold;
Let us bring Him silver and gold,
Let us bring Him silver and gold.

Said the king to the people ev'rywhere,
Listen to what I say!

Pray for peace, people ev'rywhere,
Listen to what I say!
The Child, the Child, sleeping in the night;
He will bring us goodness and light,
He will bring us goodness and light.

"I HEARD THE BELLS ON CHRISTMAS DAY"

Henry Wadsworth Longfellow, this poem's author, was born in Portland, Maine, in 1807. He graduated from Bowdoin College in 1825, where a fellow classmate was Nathaniel Hawthorne. Longfellow spent most of his professional life as a professor and librarian, and he traveled widely and wrote numerous books.

He was immensely popular during his lifetime. His narrative poems "Evangeline," "Hiawatha," and "Tales of a Wayside Inn" were favorably received by critics and the reading public alike. When "The Courtship of Miles Standish" was published in 1858, it sold more than fifteen thousand copies during the first day it was available in Boston and London.

Longfellow received honorary degrees from Oxford and Cambridge and was received in a private audience by Queen Victoria. After his death in 1882, he became the only American honored with a bust in the Poet's Corner at Westminster Abbey.

Longfellow was no stranger to sorrow. His first wife died in 1835, just four years after their wedding. His second wife was burned to death when candles in their Cambridge,

Massachusetts, home ignited her clothing in 1861. They did have eighteen happy years together and were parents of five children, but he was inconsolable in his grief.

Longfellow's bereavement was accentuated when his son, Charles, was gravely wounded during the Civil War. It was that sorrow that led to his writing the poem, "Christmas Bells," a year later. It was set to music and known as "I Heard the Bells on Christmas Day."

There is a certain melancholy in the opening verse, a wistful remembrance of things past. The refrain, "Of peace on earth, good will to men," sets the tone of this deeply antiwar poem. The poet hears the bells playing the "old familiar carols" on Christmas Day, promising peace on earth, as did the angels at the first Christmas. But immediately his thoughts turn to despair as he realizes that there is no peace and that human hatred has once again destroyed the age-old dream of peace and brotherhood.

A note of hopefulness and triumphant idealism returns in the sixth stanza as the bells peal "more loud and deep" because "God is not dead, nor doth He sleep," a memorable evocation of faith in the ultimate triumph of righteousness. "The wrong shall fail, the right prevail," the author proclaims.

Longfellow clearly identified the Union cause as synonymous with right and the Confederate cause as totally evil, which made his poem highly unpopular in the South. Stanzas reflecting these sentiments were soon removed from the musical version, which was written in 1872.

An English musician, John Baptiste Calkin, composed the most widely used tune for "I Heard the Bells." It has a kind of solemn majesty, a reflective quality, and a hint of sadness that make this carol stand out from many others. It is a paean to idealism, a plea for peace, and a song of hope in a world too often enveloped in darkness and despair. Johnny Marks also composed a snappier, more light-hearted tune, which is often heard.

"I Heard the Bells on Christmas Day"

I heard the bells on Christmas day,
Their old familiar carols play:
And wild and sweet the words repeat,
Of peace on earth, good will to men.

I thought, how as now this day had come,
The belfries of all Christendom
Had rung so long the unbroken song
Of peace on earth, good will to men.

And in despair, I bowed my head,
"There is no peace on earth," I said,
"For hate is strong and mocks the song
Of peace on earth, good will to men."

Then from each black, accursed mouth
The cannon thundered in the South,
And with the sound the carols drowned
Of peace on earth, good will to men.

It was as if an earthquake rent
The hearth-stones of a continent,
And made forlorn, the households born
Of peace on earth, good will to men.

Then pealed the bells more loud and deep,
"God is not dead, nor doth He sleep,
The wrong shall fail, the right prevail,
With peace on earth, good will to men."

Till, ringing, singing on its way,
The world revolved from night to day,
A voice, a chime, a chant sublime,
Of peace on earth, good will to men.

Note: The fourth and fifth stanzas are the offensive ones and they, along with the seventh stanza, are often omitted today.

"IT CAME UPON THE MIDNIGHT CLEAR"

Edmund Hamilton Sears, born in 1810 in the village of Sandisfield in the Berkshire Hills of western Massachusetts, was one of those quiet men whose lives are measured in the enduring calm of plains and meadows, as opposed to peaks and valleys. One of his ancestors had been among the original Pilgrims who settled in Plymouth in the early seventeenth century.

Except for his college years at Union College in Schenectady, New York, Sears spent his entire life in small Massachusetts towns. After briefly studying law, he changed career plans and entered Harvard Divinity School, graduating in 1837. He was ordained to the Unitarian ministry and held four pastorates during his lifetime. It is said he had no ambition to pastor large or influential city churches but was content as a rural parson.

Sears wrote a number of religious books and coedited a religious magazine. He rarely traveled, but a trip to England in 1873 was a signal delight for he was well known in his denominational circles and drew large crowds to his sermons.

Nineteenth-century New England Unitarians were much more conservative than their brethren would be a century later, and Sears wrote frequently about his belief in the divinity of Christ. It may be of some interest that two other Unitarian hymn writers of that century were Sarah Flower Adams, author of "Nearer My God to Thee," and Sir John Bowring, who wrote "In the Cross of Christ I Glory."

Sears is best remembered today for his lovely carol "It Came Upon the Midnight Clear," written in 1849 and first appearing in the magazine *Christian Register*. The *Christian Register*'s editor, a fellow clergyman, wrote some time later, "I always feel that, however poor my Christmas sermon may be, the reading and singing of this hymn are enough to make up for all deficiencies."

This carol shows the author's skillful use of poetry and imagery, as in "harps of gold," "the world in solemn stillness lay," and a reference to God as "heaven's all-gracious King."

The second stanza is highly descriptive of the angelic choir, while the third and fifth stanzas take on an almost polit-

ical tone, with descriptions and intimations of a future golden age of peace. Those who suffer injustice are encouraged to "hear the angels sing." This emphasis on angels explains why this carol was often called "The Blessed Angels Sing."

The music for Sears's poem was written by Richard Storrs Willis, a journalist and musician born in 1819. Willis was a Yale graduate who lived in New York, edited *Musical World* magazine, and wrote books on church music and related subjects. He studied music in Germany, where the great composer Felix Mendelssohn was one of his teachers. After he returned to New York, he became a music critic for the *New York Tribune*. While a member of the vestry at the Episcopal Church of the Transfiguration (better known as "the Little Church Around the Corner") Willis wrote the music to "It Came Upon the Midnight Clear."

Interestingly, Sears wrote an earlier Christmas carol when he was just twenty-four years old. Entitled "Calm on the List'ning Ear of Night," it was published in the *Boston Observer* in 1835 and was praised by Oliver Wendell Holmes as "one of the finest and most beautiful ever written." The lines bear a good measure of similarity to his more famous carol. It reads:

"Calm on the List'ning Ear of Night"

Calm on the list'ning ear of night
Come heaven's melodious strains,
Where wild Judea stretches forth
Her silver-mantled plains;
Celestial choirs from courts above
shed sacred glories there;
And angels, with their sparkling lyres,
Make music on the air.

The answering hills of Palestine
Send back the glad reply,
And greet from all their holy heights

The Dayspring from on high:
O'er the blue depths of Galilee
There comes a holier calm;
And Sharon waves in solemn praise
Her silent groves of palm.

"Glory to God!" the lofty strain
The realm of ether fills;
How sweeps the song of solemn joy
O'er Judah's sacred hills!
"Glory to God!" the sounding skies
Loud with their anthems ring:
"Peace on the earth; good will to men,"
From heaven's eternal King.

This day shall Christian tongues be mute,
And Christian hearts be cold?
O catch the anthem that from heaven
O'er Judah's mountains rolled,
When burst upon that listening night
The high and solemn lay,
"Glory to God; on earth be peace":
Salvation comes today.

This early carol was set to music by John Edgar Gould, a composer and author of eight books of religious and secular songs. Gould, who died in Algiers in 1875, wrote the music for the sailor's hymn, "Savior, Pilot Me."

Sears lived out his life as a country pastor. His books,

Sermons and Songs of the Christian Life, Regeneration, Foregleams of Immortality, and *The Fourth Gospel, the Heart of Christ* were widely read in his day and are now forgotten. He died in January 1876 at the age of sixty-five. While his books are forgotten, his carol "It Came Upon the Midnight Clear" is still sung and admired a century and a half after it appeared. In fact, the eminent scholar Alfred Edward Bailey, writing in his 1950 classic *The Gospel in Hymns*, made this observation, "No Christmas is perfect without the singing of this hymn. It is one of the finest ever written, not only because of its melodious rendering of the biblical story of angels and shepherds, but because it is one of the first to emphasize the social significance of the angels' message."

"It Came Upon the Midnight Clear"

It came upon the midnight clear,
That glorious song of old,
From angels bending near the earth,
To touch their harps of gold:
"Peace on the earth, good will to men,
From heaven's all gracious King":
The world in solemn stillness lay
To hear the angels sing.

Still through the cloven skies they come
With peaceful wings unfurled,

And still their heavenly music floats
O'er all the weary world;
Above its sad and lowly plains
They bend on hovering wing,
And ever o'er its Babel sounds
The blessed angels sing.

Yet with the woes of sin and strife
The world hath suffered long;
Beneath the angel-strain had rolled
Two thousand years of wrong;
And man, at war with man, hears not
The love song which they bring:
O hush the noise, ye men of strife,
And hear the angels sing.

O ye, beneath life's crushing load,
Whose forms are bending low,
Who toil along the climbing way
With painful steps and slow;
Look now! for glad and golden hours
Come swiftly on the wing;
O rest beside the weary road,
And hear the angels sing!

For lo! the days are hastening on
By prophets seen of old,
When with the ever-circling years
Shall come the time foretold;

When peace shall over all the earth
Its ancient splendors fling,
And the whole world send back the song
Which now the angels sing.

"THE LITTLE DRUMMER BOY"

This Christmas carol is unique in several respects. Its most distinctive quality is undoubtedly the drumbeat, which has always appealed to those who love songs with a strong rhythmic beat. Because of this characteristic, it is more reminiscent of European songs. After all, there is a drumlike beat to "Patapan," a French folk carol that is nearly three centuries old. Drummers are mentioned also in the English folk song "The Twelve Days of Christmas," where "the drummers drumming" are assigned to the twelfth day.

This touching song appeared in 1941 in America. Its author was Katherine K. Davis, who was born in Saint Joseph, Missouri, on January 25, 1892. Davis studied piano under Nadia Boulanger, taught piano at Wellesley College, received an honorary doctorate from Florida's Stetson University, and won an ASCAP (American Society of Composers, Artists, and Publishers) award in 1969. Before her death in 1980, Miss Davis wrote over a thousand choral works, including settings of William Blake's poems "The Lamb" and "The Tiger." She wrote a symphonic poem called "The Burial of a Queen" and an opera, *Cinderella*. Her many sacred cantatas include "This Is Noel," "Easter Is a Song," "Fanfare for Palm Sunday," and "Road to Galilee."

Davis is best remembered for her "Carol of the Drum," as she called it. In some respects this carol is similar to Gian-Carlo Menotti's opera, *Amahl and the Night Visitors*, since both tell the tales of young boys, either poor or physically handicapped, who want to bring a gift to the Christ Child. Since they have virtually nothing of this world's goods to offer, they give all that they do have. Amahl gives his crutch and is miraculously healed. The little drummer boy plays his drum for the "newborn King" and is rewarded with a smile.

The little drummer boy knows that he is poor and can give nothing more than his song, but he also believes that "it is fit to give our King." With Mary's permission and the support of the ox and lamb, who "kept time," he "played his best." It is a quiet and gentle moral message.

Davis's song may be a retelling of legends found in many European countries, where stories arose about young, poor, or marginalized members of society who offer their humble and heartfelt gifts to the baby Jesus. In France "The Juggler of Notre Dame" gave his only gift, the ability to juggle with perfection, to the Christ Child, receiving a blessing and eternal peace as his reward. In Spain and Italy, gifts are as simple as olive branches and onions. These tender legends may have influenced Davis.

The carol was given a new lease on life in 1958 when it was renamed "The Little Drummer Boy" by Harry Simeone, a onetime choral conductor with Fred Waring and the Pennsylvanians, and his collaborator Henry Onorati. The Harry Simeone Chorale version took the country by storm that Christmas, becoming the second most popular Christmas song (after "White Christmas") since 1940.

It was the thirteenth most popular song of all the thousands recorded in 1958 and remained on the lists through 1962. It was recorded by singers as diverse as Joan Baez, Johnny Cash, Emmylou Harris, Johnny Mathis, and Lou Rawls. "The Little Drummer Boy" was President Richard Nixon's favorite Christmas carol, according to the researchers who assisted Burl Ives in the production of his lively Caedmon record of 1972, *Christmas in the White House*.

Television has added to the continuing popularity of this carol. Academy Award-winning actress Greer Garson narrated a special program in 1967 on "The Little Drummer Boy." A sequel was telecast nine years later.

The popularity of "The Little Drummer Boy" seems assured for future generations.

"The Little Drummer Boy"

Come they told me
Pa rum pum pum pum.
A newborn King to see
Pa rum pum pum pum.

Our finest gifts we bring
Pa rum pum pum pum.
To lay before the king
Pa rum pum pum pum

Rum pum pum pum
Rum pum pum pum.

So to honor Him
Pa rum pum pum pum
When we come.

Little baby,
Pa rum pum pum pum.
I am a poor boy too,
Pa rum pum pum pum.
I have no gift to bring,
Pa rum pum pum pum
That's fit to give our King
Pa rum pum pum pum
Rum pum pum pum
Rum pum pum pum.

Shall I play for you
Pa rum pum pum pum
On my drum.

Mary nodded
Pa rum pum pum pum.
The ox and lamb kept time,
Pa rum pum pum pum.
I played my drum for Him
Pa rum pum pum pum.
I played my best for Him

Pa rum pum pum pum
Rum pum pum pum
Rum pum pum pum.

Then he smiled at me
Pa rum pum pum pum
Me and my drum.

"O LITTLE TOWN OF BETHLEHEM"

The first two lines of "O Little Town of Bethlehem" convey a message of peace, tranquillity, and a sense of the eternal. The contrast between "dark streets" and "the everlasting light" immediately catches our attention.

A sense of history and author Phillips Brooks's belief in the incarnation of the Son of God are conveyed in the fourth line of the first stanza, which refers to "the hopes and fears of all the years" being caught up or "met" in the birth of Christ. All five stanzas are rich in history, symbolism, and a kind of tenderhearted theology that appeals to people of all ages.

It is perhaps unsurprising that its author was a man of the cloth whose sermons were so well received that they often became public events in nineteenth-century America. Brooks was Boston-born and Harvard-educated. He had, as was often remarked, good prospects for a successful life, owing to the advantages of his childhood. But it took a while for young Brooks to find his niche. As a professor of Latin in the famed Boston Latin School, which he had attended as a youth for five years, he was a failure. The ministry was what suited him best. It was his destiny.

Brooks had always been a scholarly young man, graduating third in his class at Boston Latin and entering Harvard at the age of sixteen. Brooks left Boston in October 1856 for the Virginia Theological Seminary to prepare for the Episcopal priesthood. He was ordained in 1859 and spent the next ten years at two Philadelphia parishes, the Church of the Advent and the Church of the Holy Trinity, the latter a prominent parish on fashionable Rittenhouse Square.

Brooks's forte was preaching, and people were attracted to his sermons by his eloquence and sincerity. He took a special interest in ministering to Union soldiers during the Civil War and he called President Abraham Lincoln's Emancipation Proclamation "the greatest and most glorious thing our land has ever seen."

It was during his days at Holy Trinity that "O Little Town of Bethlehem" was born. Brooks was physically exhausted from his strenuous activity during the war years, and Holy Trinity granted him a year's leave of absence with full salary from July 1865 to July 1866. He spent most of it in Europe, arriving in the Holy Land just before the Christmas of 1865. He and his party rode on horseback for the two-hour journey to Bethlehem. The little town left an indelible impression on his memory, as did a five-hour worship service at the Church of the Nativity, which is traditionally said to be on the very spot of the holy birth. Brooks kept a detailed diary of his experiences.

It has long been argued that Brooks did not write "O Little Town" until three years later in Philadelphia, but that may be an error perpetuated by numerous writers. Brooks's noted biographer, church historian Raymond W. Albright, wrote, "It is now almost certain that Brooks wrote his hymn 'O Little Town of Bethlehem' that night in or near those fields in Bethlehem, just as on other occasions when deeply moved he wrote his best poetry." An early biographer, A. V. G. Allen also asserts this in his many-volumed *Life and Letters of Phillips Brooks*, published in 1900 and 1901. Allen interviewed a companion on the journey who told him that Brooks had written the poem "on the spot," something Brooks appeared to have corroborated in a letter to Lucy Larcom (a popular novelist of the day) dated December 28, 1886.

Whenever it was written, the poem became a hymn in a rather extraordinary way. Brooks had customarily prepared an original carol for the Christmas services at his parish Sunday school class. In 1868 he gave a copy of "O Little Town" to his organist Lewis H. Redner and asked Redner to write the music. Redner, a businessman and Sunday school superintendent, could not find the time or inspiration for the task. As Christmas approached, he had still not written a line of music. Then something quite unexpected occurred. Writes Raymond Albright: "Redner had little success in preparing an appropriate tune until the night before rehearsal when he was 'roused from sleep late in the night hearing an angel strain whispering in my ear.' He jotted down at once the melody and the next morning before church filled in the harmony. The children at Holy Trinity learned it eagerly and sang it regularly each Christmastide but it was to be at least a decade until the well-loved hymn was widely known and sung."

In later years, Brooks was a bit bemused by the lavish attention given to "O Little Town." In a letter to author Lucy

Larcom, he confessed, "It has been printed in hymn books and sung at a good many Christmases. Where the newspapers found it all of a sudden I do not know."

This was the last Christmas for Brooks in Philadelphia, as he was called to be rector of old and historic Trinity Church in Boston in 1869. Brooks, who never married, became nationally celebrated for his sermons at Trinity until his death at the age of fifty-seven in 1893.

Brooks was so admired that the day of his funeral, January 26, 1893, was designated an official day of mourning in Massachusetts. Stores were closed as was the Stock Exchange. Thousands passed by his bier at Trinity Church on Copley Square. His honorary pallbearers included President Charles Eliot of Harvard University, Justice Horace Gray of the United States Supreme Court, and best-selling novelist Weir Mitchell.

The Presiding Bishop of the Episcopal Church officiated at the service, and long lines of mourners greeted his funeral cortege as it made its way to Mount Auburn Cemetery across the Charles River in Cambridge.

Brooks was devoted to Christmas as a festival of the Church. He wrote numerous Christmas poems and carols, including "Christmas Once is Christmas Still." His "Christmas Sermon" received national acclaim in *Century Magazine* in December 1893. A decade after Brooks's death. his book *Christmas Songs and Easter Carols* was published. An essay, "A Constant Christmas," appeared in 1890.

Brooks wrote two other carols that were once popular. In 1961 Christmas historian Daniel Foley claimed that "everyone who loves Christmas knows a few lines of 'Everywhere, Everywhere, Christmas Tonight,'" a poem-carol by Brooks. It celebrates the universality of the Christmas message with such lines as:

> *For the Christ-child who comes is the Master of all,*
> *No place too great and no cottage too small;*
> *The angels who welcome Him sing from the height,*
> *In the City of David a King in His might.*

In "The Voice of the Christ-Child," Brooks became more reflective and meditative. He reminds his listeners that the child of Bethlehem came for "the sad and the lonely, the wretched and poor," offering hope to those who "dared not dream of it before." His opening stanza sings out, "The earth has grown old with its burden of care, but at Christmas it always is young." And he closes with these thoughts:

> *The feet of the humblest may walk in the field*

> *Where the feet of the holiest have trod,*
> *This, this is the marvel to mortals revealed,*
> *When the silvery trumpets of Christmas have pealed,*
> *That mankind are the children of God.*

Still, it is his lovely recollection of that first Christmas in Bethlehem that is no longer just enjoyed by one Sunday school class in Philadelphia, but by people all over the world.

On the centennial of its first appearance, the prestigious weekly magazine, *Christian Century*, editorialized that "O Little Town" will live forever because it is "a carol which is perfect in its simplicity and wonder."

"O Little Town of Bethlehem"

> *O little town of Bethlehem,*
> *How still we see thee lie!*
> *Above thy deep and dreamless sleep*
> *The silent stars go by;*
> *Yet in thy dark streets shineth*
> *The everlasting Light;*
> *The hopes and fears of all the years*
> *Are met in thee tonight.*
>
> *For Christ is born of Mary,*
> *And gathered all above,*
> *While mortals sleep, the angels keep*
> *Their watch of wondering love.*
> *O morning stars, together*

Proclaim the holy birth,
And praises sing to God the King,
And peace to men on earth!

How silently, how silently,
The wondrous Gift is given!
So God imparts to human hearts
The blessings of His heaven.
No ear may hear His coming,
But in this world of sin,
Where meek souls will receive Him, still
The dear Christ enters in.

O holy Child of Bethlehem,
Descend to us, we pray;
Cast out our sin, and enter in,
Be born in us today.
We hear the Christmas angels
The great glad tidings tell;
O come to us, abide with us,
Our Lord Immanuel!

"There's a Song in the Air"

Both Josiah Holland, the author of the words, and Karl Harrington, the composer, contributed unique insights to the development of this inviting carol.

Holland, born in Massachusetts in 1819, was a high school dropout who dabbled in photography and calligraphy before completing his education and entering medical school. He then practiced medicine for a number of years before deciding to become the owner and editor of a newspaper. His search for a meaningful and fulfilling professional life ended when he entered the literary world, remaining there until his death in 1882.

Holland wrote numerous novels and poems in addition to his editorial projects. He was longtime editor of the *Springfield Republican* and became the first editor of *Scribner's Monthly*, a popular high-class journal, in 1870. James D. Hart's *Oxford Companion to American Literature* says of Holland, "His many books were popular in their day, being well suited to the homely taste for sentimental didacticism."

A classic Victorian author, Holland emphasized virtue and moral principles in his novels, which were always centered around strong individuals fighting the temptation to depart from the straight and narrow. Holland also wrote serious volumes of poetry and admonitions to young readers.

"There's a Song in the Air" appeared in Holland's 1872 book *The Marble Prophecy and Other Poems*. It begins quietly and softly, building up to the nativity event. The last line in each of the four stanzas refers to the Christ child as a king. He has a fondness for the words "fire" and "aflame," which seems slightly out of character with the coolness of the poem in general. His reference to "the beautiful sing" is also a bit puzzling.

The poem proved popular among readers, and it was included in Holland's *Complete Poetical Writings*. More than three decades later, a scholarly Latin professor at Wesleyan University, who also wrote hymns and other musical compositions, turned this little poem into a melodic Christmas song. Karl Harrington, whose father had been an editor of a Methodist hymnal, spent his summers at a cottage in North Woodstock, New Hampshire. In July 1904 Harrington sat down at his organ and composed the music for Holland's poem. The fact that it was in midsummer did not seem to deter Harrington.

Harrington also wrote the music for a number of other Christmas songs, including "While Shepherds Watched Their Flocks by Night" and the completely forgotten "Long Years Ago O'er Bethlehem's Hills." Harrington's music for "The Lord Is in His Holy Temple, Let All the Earth Keep Silence Before Him" is occasionally used today.

Both Holland and Harrington were such deep-dyed New Englanders that this song was often called "The New England Carol."

"There's a Song in the Air"

There's a song in the air!
There's a star in the sky!
There's a mother's deep prayer,
And a baby's low cry!
And the star rains its fire while the beautiful sing,
For the manger of Bethlehem cradles a King!

There's a tumult of joy
O'er the wonderful birth,

For the Virgin's sweet boy
Is the Lord of the earth.
Ay! the star rains its fire while the beautiful sing,
For the manger of Bethlehem cradles a King!

In the light of that star
Lie the ages impearled;
And that song from afar
Has swept over the world.
Every hearth is aflame, and the beautiful sing
In the homes of the nations that Jesus is King!

We rejoice in the light,
And we echo the song
That comes down through the night
From the heavenly throng.
Ay! we shout to the lovely evangel they bring,
And we greet in His cradle, our Saviour and King!

"WE THREE KINGS OF ORIENT ARE"

Beginning with its first stanza, this delightful carol exudes the exotic fragrance of faraway places. It is one of the rare carols that celebrates the coming of the Magi to worship the newborn King. The motif of the star also stands out prominently in the opening lines and in the refrain.

The music even suggests the onward movement of caravans traversing great distances through difficult terrain. It has been suggested that one reason for the carol's enduring

popularity has been the interest of Americans who love to travel to far-off places and, in particular, the appeal of pilgrimages to the Holy Land. This wanderlust was accentuated by improvements in transportation, communication, and education in mid-nineteenth-century America, about the time this song first appeared.

The second, third, and fourth stanzas are designed to be sung by each of the three kings bearing gifts (of gold, frankincense, and myrrh). The verse referring to myrrh alludes to the crucifixion and death of Jesus, with its stark use of such words as "bitter perfume," "gathering gloom," and "stone-cold tomb." The closing stanza restores the note of joy at the beginning by referring to the Resurrection.

This many-layered and textured carol was written by John Henry Hopkins Jr., probably in 1857, as a Christmas present from the lifelong bachelor to his nieces and nephews.

Hopkins, born in Pittsburgh in 1820, had a varied career. His parents were immigrants—his father from Dublin and his mother from Hamburg. He graduated from the University of Vermont in 1839 and became a reporter for a New York City newspaper while also attending law school. He then decided to prepare for the ministry and entered the General Theological Seminary in New York's Chelsea district (where Clement Clarke Moore, author of "A Visit From Saint Nicholas," taught for many years) and was ordained a deacon in 1850. Instead of proceeding directly to the priesthood, Hopkins decided to edit a religious magazine that he called *Church Journal*. He also became the first instructor in church music ever employed by the seminary.

In his spare time Hopkins designed stained glass windows, dabbled in church architecture and furnishings, and wrote hymns and carols. His 1863 book *Carols, Hymns, and Songs* included the first publication of "We Three Kings of Orient Are." He also wrote the words to "Come With Us, O Blessed Jesus" and the music to "Come, Holy Ghost, Our Souls Inspire." Hopkins's biographer, Charles Sweet, called him "one of the most accomplished hymnologists in the United States."

Hopkins was finally ordained a priest in 1872, twenty-two years after becoming a deacon, and served parishes in Plattsburgh, New York, and Williamsport, Pennsylvania. He was a hard-working rural parson who traveled miles on primitive roads to establish missions among Central Pennsylvania's rural folk. After being hit by a Broadway horse car (equivalent to being run over by a taxi today), Hopkins's health deteriorated and he died at a friend's home near Hudson, New York, on August 14, 1891.

"We Three Kings of Orient Are" took a while to reach popular acclaim. It was not added to the *Episcopal Hymnal* until 1916, when "carols" were first officially sanctioned for use in Episcopal worship. Christmas "hymns" were sung, however. The *Methodist Hymnal* added the carol in 1935.

The Episcopalians declared "We Three Kings of Orient Are" an Epiphany carol. The feast of the Epiphany on January 6 became a church holy day in the third century. Epiphany is a Greek word that means "the manifestation of Christ to the gentiles." It celebrated the coming of the Magi, who are mentioned only in the first twelve verses of the second chapter of

Matthew's Gospel. The original text in Matthew does not enumerate how many Magi there were.

In Eastern Orthodox Christianity the feast is generally called Theophany. Epiphany is observed in the calendars of the Roman Catholic, Episcopal, Lutheran, and Eastern Orthodox churches, and is now being celebrated by many other Christian churches as well. It is an official legal holiday in twenty-one nations, including Austria, Italy, Spain, Greece, Finland, Switzerland, Germany, and Sweden. In Latin America and Spain it is called Three Kings Day.

Shakespeare's play *Twelfth Night* occurs at Epiphany, and T. S. Eliot's "Journey of the Magi" is considered one of the great poems of the twentieth century. (Eliot based his poem on a seventeenth-century Christmas sermon by Lancelot Andrewes.)

"We Three Kings of Orient Are" is frequently sung in Sunday school pageants during the Christmas season. For many years it was the processional hymn during the "Festival of Lights," held on the Sunday evening nearest Epiphany, at Saint John's Cathedral in Jacksonville, Florida.

Most scholars believe that the Magi were probably astrologers who lived in Persia, not members of a royal family. Stephen J. Binz, a recent biblical scholar, explains: "The word *Magi* originally referred to a Persian priestly caste noted for their interpretation of dreams. Later it came to refer to any possessors of supernatural knowledge and power. Here they are probably astrologers who look to the movement by stars as a guide to human events and destiny."

The popular religious imagination of the Middle Ages

came to identify the three mysterious visitors with kings and gave them the names Caspar, Balthazar, and Melchior. Their gifts of gold, frankincense, and myrrh were given symbolic and mystical meanings.

By the time crèches and Nativity scenes became a popular art form, the Three Kings tradition was well established. The day is a popular gift-giving day in Italy, Portugal, Spain, and Latin America.

It was this tradition that Hopkins drew upon when he came to write this carol nearly a century and a half ago.

Hopkins also wrote the words and music for a charming if now forgotten carol, "Gather Around the Christmas Tree." It includes the lovely verse,

Christ our King is born today!
His reign shall never pass away.
Hosanna, Hosanna, Hosanna in the highest!

"We Three Kings of Orient Are"

We three kings of Orient are,
Bearing gifts we traverse afar,
Field and fountain, moor and mountain,
Following yonder star.

(Refrain:)
O star of wonder, star of night,
Star with royal beauty bright;

Westward leading, still proceeding,
Guide us to thy perfect light!

Born a King on Bethlehem's plain
Gold I bring to crown him again,
King forever, ceasing never
Over us all to reign.

(Refrain)

Frankincense to offer have I;
Incense owns a Deity nigh;
Prayer and praising all men raising,
Worship him, God on high.

(Refrain)

Myrrh is mine; its bitter perfume
Breathes a life of gathering gloom;
Sorrowing, sighing, bleeding, dying,
Sealed in a stone-cold tomb.

(Refrain)

Glorious now behold him arise,
King and God and Sacrifice;
Alleluia, Alleluia!
Sounds through the earth and skies.

(Refrain)

IV

PUT ON YOUR
DANCING SHOES

Dancing has long been a part of Christmas celebrations, from "Mr. Fezziwig's ball" in Charles Dickens to the cotillions of the Old South. A popular English carol named "Tomorrow Shall Be My Dancing Day" expresses joy at both the birth of Christ and the festive nature of the season. It also refers to the mystical marriage between Christ and his "true love," the Church.

Dance carols were popular during the Middle Ages. Sacred dance was performed, and still is at certain times, in the Cathedral in Seville, Spain. In York Minster in northern England, choir boys danced in the aisles after divine services on Christmas Day.

An Austrian carol brings mirth to the season:

> *Bring your pipes and bring your drum,*
> *Call the shepherds all to come.*
> *Hasten, quick, no time to lose.*
> *Don't forget your dancing shoes.*

The carol also addresses the Christ child:

Jesus dearest, Thee to greet,
Hasten we with dancing feet.

In this section, we include three examples of American popular songs with dance themes—a waltz and two rock songs.

"THE CHRISTMAS WALTZ"

Sammy Cahn and Jule Styne, who gave us "Let It Snow" nearly a decade before, again collaborated for "The Christmas Waltz," which appeared in 1954.

"The Christmas Waltz" is a rare example of a carol written especially for dancing or gliding across an icy pond. The song tinkles with Christmas images of "frosted window panes," "gleaming candles," and "painted candy canes." "It's that time of year when the world falls in love," they claim, and it is, of course, the time when "Santa's on his way" with "a sleigh filled with things for you and me." It's a happy song, complete with a hope that everyone's "New Year dreams come true."

In his book *I Should Care: The Sammy Cahn Story*, Cahn tells how "The Christmas Waltz" came to be written. Los Angeles was in the middle of a hot spell when he received a phone call from Jule Styne telling him that Frank Sinatra wanted them to compose a Christmas song for him. Cahn was hesitant to do a Christmas song because he didn't see how they could compete with Berlin's "White Christmas." But Styne insisted that they give Sinatra what he wanted, so they got together at Styne's apartment. Styne always warmed up with a tango and a waltz. It gave Cahn the idea that a Christmas waltz might be unique. He told Styne to play his waltz again and then kept asking him to slow it down a little as he began writing the words to what would become "The Christmas Waltz."

Cahn said that he "agonized" over an "impure rhyme" of the words mine and time in the lyric, "And this song of mine, In three-quarter time." He tried and rejected several lines in trying to find just the right words to rhyme with "In three-quarter time," including: "And the sleigh bells chime," "And this little rhyme," "And this song sublime." Finally he settled on his original line even though it wasn't perfect. Cahn said, "We decided to let "The Christmas Waltz" be only 99 and 44/100 percent pure."

Both Lawrence Welk and Frank Sinatra did well with the record-buying public in recording this song.

"The Christmas Waltz"

Frosted window panes, candles gleaming inside,
Painted candy canes on the tree;
Santa's on his way, he's filled his sleigh with things,
Things for you and for me.

It's that time of year, when the world falls in love,
Ev'ry song you hear seems to say:

"Merry Christmas, may your New Year dreams come true."
And this song of mine, in three-quarter time,
Wishes you and yours the same thing too.

"JINGLE-BELL ROCK"

Rock music doesn't suit everyone's taste, but it emerged in the 1950s as an amalgamation of earlier styles and rhythms that had appealed to younger generations.

"Jingle-Bell Rock" became a surprise hit in 1957, the number-one Christmas song of that memorable year of Sputnik and Little Rock. In fact, the version by twenty-one-year-old Bobby Helms is the third most popular Christmas song since 1940, according to researcher Craig Pattillo.

In a 1990 interview Helms recalled that he was unsure about whether Christmas and rock 'n' roll would meld as a concept. But this song, the first one to employ rock in the service of Christmas, proved popular. Ironically, it was written one hundred years after "Jingle Bells." Helms, who died in Martinsville, Indiana, on June 19, 1997, also had hits with "My Special Angel" and "Fraulein" before turning to nightclub activities and music festivals later in his life.

The co-authors of "Jingle-Bell Rock" were Joseph Beal and James R. Boothe, who were involved primarily with public relations, advertising, and reporting. They were not well-known musicians or lyricists, but their words are catchy and fun.

Another version of the song, by Bobby Rydell and Chubby Checker, was the number-one Christmas song of 1961.

"Jingle-Bell Rock"

Jingle bell, jingle bell, jingle bell rock,
Jingle bells swing and jingle bells ring.
Snowing and blowing up bushels of fun,
Now the jingle hop has begun.

Jingle bell, jingle bell, jingle bell rock,
Jingle bells chime in jingle bell time.
Dancing and prancing in Jingle Bell Square,
In the frosty air.

What a bright time, it's the right time
To rock the night away.
Jingle bell time is a swell time,
To go gliding in a one-horse sleigh.

Giddy-up jungle horse, pick up your feet,
Jingle around the clock.
Mix and a-mingle in the jingling feet,
That's the jingle bell
That's the jingle bell,
That's the jingle bell rock.

"ROCKIN' AROUND THE CHRISTMAS TREE"

Johnny Marks, an incredibly versatile composer of Christmas tunes, added to the popularity of rock music with this 1958 composition. Marks is addressing the relatively well-behaved teenagers of the 1950s who are enjoying a "Christmas party hop" with caroling, mistletoe, and pumpkin pie. A certain harmless innocence and merriness are conveyed, while the last line refers to the new dancing style as a "new old fashioned way," a way of noting that while dancing styles change, they have a tendency to become old hat rather soon.

Brenda Lee made this the most popular Christmas song of 1960 and the seventh most popular of all time. Lee, born in Lithonia, Georgia, in 1944, has been singing since she won a talent contest at the age of five. In 1955 "Little Miss Dynamite" appeared on Red Foley's *Ozark Jubilee* television show and the following year signed a contract with Decca Records. In the 1960s Lee blended country and rock styles to become a popular performer, with such hits as "I'm Sorry," "All Alone Am I," and "Break It To Me Gently." Still a world-renowned touring artist, Lee signed with Warner Brothers Records in 1991.

"Rockin' Around the Christmas Tree"

Rockin' around the Christmas tree
At the Christmas party hop.
Mistletoe hung where you can see
Every couple tries to stop.

Rockin' around the Christmas tree,
Let the Christmas spirit ring.

Later we'll have some pumpkin pie
And we'll do some caroling.

You will get a sentimental feeling
When you hear voices singing,
"Let's be jolly,
Deck the halls with boughs of holly."

Rockin' around the Christmas tree,
Have a happy holiday.
Everyone dancing merrily
In the new old fashioned way.

SANTA CLAUS
AND FRIENDS

The American Santa Claus, whose visual persona is largely the creation of nineteenth-century magazine and book illustrator Thomas Nast, has been featured in many songs of the holiday season. Children instinctively identify with the large man in the red suit, with a white beard and rotund belly. It is hard to imagine Christmas without this jovial bearer of gifts.

Christmas somehow managed to get celebrated for about nineteen centuries before Santa Claus came along. Stories of his origin are varied, but many seem to agree that Santa Claus is based on the legends surrounding Saint Nicholas, a kindly bishop of Myra (in present-day Turkey) in the fourth century. Nicholas endured the persecution of Christians under emperor Diocletian and may have attended the ecumenical council of Nicaea, an important church gathering held in the year 325. His years as bishop were noted for his charity and kindness, especially to widows, orphans, the poor, and the least-regarded members of society.

His death on December 6 (presumably in 341), was soon observed as a saint's day in the church calendars, East and West. Several hundred churches were named for him, and he became the patron saint of Greece and Russia. In the West, he was most popular in Holland, Belgium, Switzerland, Germany, and Austria.

Saint Nicholas was considered the gift-giver for good and well-behaved children, to whom he brought presents on his feast day, December 6. Bad children, however, might be given coals or switches by Belsnickel, his evil companion. This German character is remembered each year at the Landis Valley Farm Museum in Lancaster County, Pennsylvania.

Even after the Reformation, when the veneration of saints was discouraged in the Protestant world, Nicholas retained his popularity. He still came on the eve of December 6 to fill Dutch children's wooden clog shoes with toys and candies. Dutch New Yorkers in the seventeenth century made the kindly old gentleman, now known as Sinter Klaas, a part of Christmas that even many of the English settlers adopted as their own.

By mid-nineteenth-century America, "Jolly Old Saint Nicholas" had been heralded by poet Clement Clarke Moore, and by songwriters who celebrated his merry exploits. Each succeeding generation has added to the folklore of Santa Claus.

The songs selected for this section illustrate the many traditions surrounding this beloved character.

"HERE COMES SANTA CLAUS"

The great country and western singer and film actor Gene Autry wrote this perennial Christmas favorite with composer Oakley Haldeman in 1947. The simple lines, the singable tune, and the carefree air of Christmas delight make this a song that most listeners will want to hum along with or even join in singing. Autry and Haldeman wrote this song because Autry was often the grand marshal in the Hollywood Christmas Parade.

Soon after its debut, "Here Comes Santa Claus" was recorded by Autry, and it sold briskly. Singers as diverse as Doris Day, Eddie Fisher, Red Foley, Jimmy Boyd, and Bing Crosby also recorded versions of it. But Gene Autry's 1947 recording is the most popular of all, as evidenced by its gold and platinum status.

Sociologist James H. Barnett, writing in the 1950s, published a wonderfully inventive and pioneering study of the development of popular Christmas customs in America and the underlying presuppositions that they represented. In *The American Christmas: A Study in National Culture*, Barnett noted that the words to some popular Christmas songs "throw light on contemporary attitudes toward the festival." About this song he writes: " 'Here Comes Santa Claus' admonishes children to give thanks to the Lord because Santa Claus is coming to visit them. This advice is accompanied by the equalitarian assurance that Santa Claus doesn't care if they are rich or poor, for he will love them just the same."

"Here Comes Santa Claus"

Here comes Santa Claus, here comes Santa Claus
Right down Santa Claus Lane.
Vixen and Blitzen and all his reindeer,
Pulling on the reins.
Bells are ringing, children singing
All is merry and bright.
So, hang your stockings and say your prayers,
'Cause Santa Claus comes tonight.

Here comes Santa Claus, here comes Santa Claus
Right down Santa Claus Lane.
He's got a bag that's filled with toys
For boys and girls again.
Hear those sleigh bells jingle jangle,
Oh, what a beautiful sight.
So jump in bed and cover your head,
'Cause Santa Claus comes tonight.

Here comes Santa Claus, here comes Santa Claus
Right down Santa Claus Lane.
He'll come around when chimes ring out
It's Christmas time again.
Peace on earth will come to all
If we just follow the light,
So let's give thanks to the Lord above
'Cause Santa Claus comes tonight.

Here comes Santa Claus, here comes Santa Claus
Right down Santa Claus Lane.
Vixen and Blitzen and all his reindeer
Pulling on the reins.
Bells are ringing, children singing
All is merry and bright.
So jump in bed and cover your head
'Cause Santa Claus comes tonight.

Here comes Santa Claus, here comes Santa Claus
Right down Santa Claus Lane.
He doesn't care if you're rich or poor
He loves you just the same.
Santa Claus knows we're all God's children
That makes everything right.
So fill your hearts with Christmas cheer,
'Cause Santa Claus comes tonight.

"JOLLY OLD SAINT NICHOLAS"

This song is a companion to "Up on the Housetop" in more ways than one. It clearly emerged in the same period, the mid-nineteenth century. Also, its style and content suggest a Civil War or Gilded Age time frame. It may have been written by Benjamin Hanby, but most musical historians are inclined to accept its anonymity.

It's an effusive and happy tune, written in the form of a wish or an imagined conversation between a young child and the "dear old man" who brings the gifts. Skates, sleds, and picture books are mentioned as the hoped-for presents, which suggests a northern United States origin for the author. Santa's judgment in gift selection is delicately and charmingly depicted at the end of the third stanza.

Since the 1940s, the Ames Brothers, Eddy Arnold, and Montana Slim have all made recordings of "Jolly Old Saint Nicholas" that sold well.

"Jolly Old Saint Nicholas"

Jolly old Saint Nicholas,
Lean your ear this way.
Don't you tell a single soul
What I'm going to say,
Christmas Eve is coming soon,
Now, you dear old man
Whisper what you'll bring to me;
Tell me if you can.

When the clock is striking twelve,
When I'm fast asleep,
Down the chimney broad and black,
With your pack you'll creep.
All the stockings you will find
Hanging in a row.
Mine will be the shortest one,
You'll be sure to know.

Johnny wants a pair of skates;
Susy wants a sled;
Nellie wants a picture book,
Yellow, blue, and red.
Now I think I'll leave to you
What to give the rest.
Choose for me, dear Santa Claus,
You will know the best.

"OLD TOY TRAINS"

Roger Miller was one of the best multitalented composers and singers in recent America. Born in Fort Worth, Texas, in 1936 and raised "dirt poor" as he put it, near the small Oklahoma town of Erick, Miller achieved stardom as a result of his sheer talent and hard work.

After a few years, he became a national icon, winning eleven Grammy awards during 1964 and 1965. His great songs include "King of the Road," "Dang Me" (his first major hit), and "Chug-a-Lug."

He played guitar and sang for Ray Price's Cherokee Cowboys, wrote songs for Ernest Tubb and Faron Young, and collaborated with George Jones.

His humor, vitality, and irreverence were legendary. Perhaps his greatest triumph as an artist came in 1985, when he won seven Tony Awards for his Broadway musical, *Big River*, based somewhat on Mark Twain's *Huckleberry Finn*. Tragically, he died of throat cancer on October 25, 1992, at the age of fifty-six.

Miller left us with one Christmas song: "Old Toy Trains." The words are direct and simple, and they appeal to the heartstrings of the listener. They conjure up memories of the toy trains that generations of American boys received at Christmastime. Along with bicycles, red wagons, and baseball gloves, the little toy trains constituted almost prescribed gifts for male children in countless American households for decades.

Miller's few words almost seem designed to lull the excited children to sleep. Indeed, one line asks, "Little boy, don't you think it's time you were in bed?"

What makes this song doubly appealing is that it was written by Miller for his son Dean, who is following in his father's footsteps as an artist with Capitol Nashville.

Dean recalls this song as "the finest gift I've ever received." Noting that his father did not particularly relish the details of Christmas celebrations and relied on his wife Mary, Dean remembered, "Dad loved having what he considered a Norman Rockwell kind of Christmas at our house in Santa Fe. He wanted everything decorated and beautiful during the holidays, but he didn't have much to do with making it happen. Since my father was sometimes uncomfortable with the seasonal details, it became even more important to me when he gave me the finest gift I've ever received. The year I was ten years old, Dad sat down and played a song he had written just for me, a Christmas song entitled, 'Old Toy Trains.' I cherished that song and listened to him singing it on tape hundreds of times while I was growing up." He added that years later, as a sophisticated teenager with a somewhat jaded view of the holidays, he awoke to his radio playing his dad's "Old Toy Trains." Then, he says, "Whatever spirit was lagging came soaring back over the airways, compliments of my father."

"Old Toy Trains"

Old toy trains
Little toy tracks
Little toy drums coming from a sack
Carried by a man dressed in white and red
Little boy don't you think it's time you were in bed?

Close your eyes
Listen to the skies
All is calm, all is well
Soon you'll hear Kris Kringle
And the jingle bells
Bringing

Old toy trains
Little toy tracks
Little toy drums coming from a sack
Carried by a man dressed in white and red
Little boy don't you think it's time you were in bed?

"RUDOLPH THE RED-NOSED REINDEER"

This might be the only Christmas song in musical history to have begun life as an advertising venture. In early January 1939, Robert L. May, a young advertising copywriter at Montgomery Ward Company, was asked by his boss to write a short children's book for Christmas. His first effort displeased the boss so he refined it over the summer and completed it in August. He told the story of a lonely reindeer who, by virtue of his red nose, saves Santa Claus's Christmas Eve journey on a foggy night.

The boss liked this version and it was printed in an enchanting edition that reached nearly 2.5 million people. May, a 1926 Dartmouth graduate, was soft-spoken and modest. He was delighted that children all over the nation (and eventually the world) found such delight and happiness in this story. May also referred to Rudolph as "my generous son," claiming that the little fellow helped him send his six children to college. Montgomery Ward reissued the book in 1946, this time with 3.5 million copies in print.

Publishers, literary and musical, wanted to cash in on the charming tale. In 1946, Sewell Avery, the chairman of Montgomery Ward, gave the copyright to May. In 1947 a children's book publisher brought out a new edition that sold one hundred thousand copies in two years. May told friends, "Everything connected with Rudolph has a touch of miracle about it, a kindly star." He donated the original manuscript to Dartmouth College's Baker Library in 1958. May retired from Montgomery Ward in 1970 and died in 1976.

May's brother-in-law, the prolific composer Johnny Marks, adapted the story to a musical format noted for its charm, singability, and jauntiness. Marks's song resonated with a public eager to support underdogs and to see the worthy confound the wise. Rudolph's popularity enhanced the celebrity status of Marks, who delighted in composing Christmas songs of many kinds.

"Rudolph" was the second-best-selling record of all time, according to *Variety*'s December 20, 1961 issue. Only "White Christmas" has outsold it. By the mid-1960s more than forty-three million records had been sold in ninety different arrangements. ASCAP selected it in 1963 as one of the sixteen songs on the all-time Hit Parade. By the late 1970s sales had topped one hundred million.

Merchandise spin-offs and television specials enhanced its success. Folk teller and songster extraordinaire Burl Ives narrated and sang the song in a 1964 network special that has become an annual holiday-season TV treat. Twelve years later Red Skelton narrated *Rudolph's Shiny New Year*. This was followed by *Rudolph and Frosty*, which featured the voices of, among others, Ethel Merman and Mickey Rooney. A feature-length film, *Rudolph the Red-Nosed Reindeer—The Movie*, was released in 1998, featuring the voices of, among others, John Goodman, Whoopi Goldberg, Sarah Jessica Parker, and Debbie Reynolds.

Of all the versions of "Rudolph," the first one, by country western star Gene Autry, is still the one most remembered by fans. In his warm and candid autobiography, *Back in the Saddle Again*, Autry tells how he was initially reluctant to record what became his greatest hit. Two years after his "Here Comes Santa Claus" swept the country, Autry was in the market for another Christmas song that might catch the nation's fancy. He sifted through dozens of unsolicited demo records and decided on "He's a Chubby Little Fellow," "Santa, Santa, Santa," and "If It Doesn't Snow on Christmas." But he was lacking a fourth song for the two records planned that year of 1949.

Autry tells the story: "Meanwhile, a young New York song-writer named Johnny Marks had mailed me a home recording of a number called 'Rudolph the Red-Nosed Reindeer.' I played it at home that night for my wife. It not only struck me as silly but I took the position that there were already too many reindeer flying around. But to my surprise, Ina loved it. There was a line in the song about the other reindeer not letting Rudolph join in any reindeer games, and she was touched by it. 'Oh, Gene,' she said, 'it reminds me of the story of the Ugly Duckling. I think you ought to give it a try. The kids will love it.' With time running out, I reluctantly gave the demo record of 'Rudolph' to Carl Cotner, and told him to work up an arrangement. 'After all,' I said, with a shrug, 'we still have to do four songs.' "

Even the recording session was fraught with problems. "Rudolph" nearly didn't make it into the last slot. But the record finally appeared, after Gene initially introduced the song at an annual rodeo in Madison Square Garden. "Rudolph" sold two and a half million records that year, and by 1977 the Autry version alone had surpassed the ten-million mark in sales.

There is a nice postscript to this story, as related by Autry:

"It wasn't until years later that I learned, from Johnny Marks, that he had sent out demo records to Dinah Shore, Bing Crosby, and a half dozen other major artists, none of whom showed any interest. He added my name to the list as an afterthought. And, in the end, I recorded it to please my wife. All "Rudolph" did was move me out of the country class and onto the top pop charts for the first time.

"Every Christmas since 1949, Johnny calls. We chat about the latest sales figures for 'Rudolph,' and he wishes Ina and me the best of holiday greetings. He talks about 'Rudolph' as though he were real, and to Johnny he is, as our creations often tend to be."

Johnny Marks, who died in 1985, wrote a number of Christmas songs that Autry recorded, including "When Santa Claus Gets Your Letter" (1950), "The Night Before Christmas Song" (1952), "Everyone's a Child at Christmas" (1956), and "Nine Little Reindeer" (1959). Autry, America's beloved singing cowboy, died in 1998.

"Rudolph the Red-Nosed Reindeer"

You know Dasher and Dancer and Prancer and Vixen,
Comet and Cupid and Donner and Blitzen,
But do you recall the most famous reindeer of all?

Rudolph the red-nosed reindeer
Had a very shiny nose,

■

And if you ever saw it,
You would even say it glows.

All of the other reindeer
Used to laugh and call him names.
They never let poor Rudolph
Join in any reindeer games.

Then one foggy Christmas Eve,
Santa came to say:
"Rudolph, with your nose so bright,
Won't you guide my sleigh tonight?"

Then how the reindeer loved him
As they shouted out with glee:
"Rudolph the red-nosed reindeer,
You'll go down in history!"

"SANTA BABY"

This Christmas song, written by Joan Javits, Phil Springer, and Tony Springer, is clearly for "adults only," especially as it was rendered by the sensual and seductive Eartha Kitt, who made it the most popular Christmas song of 1953.

The "Santa" here is a boyfriend or sugar daddy, and there are certain implications of hanky-panky. The sentiments expressed are pure materialism. The singer, obviously a female who claims to have been "an awful good girl" and "an angel all year," gives her Santa a mind-boggling Christmas list: a sable, a 1954 light blue convertible, a yacht, a platinum mine, a duplex, an unlimited checking account, and some Tiffany Christmas tree decorations. After everyone's eyebrows have been raised by these subtle intimations, the singer/composer asks for a wedding ring, which presumably legitimated whatever has been going on!

"Santa Baby" is told to "hurry down the chimney tonight" in this sophisticated double entendre song that appeared during the first year of the Eisenhower presidency.

Eartha Kitt was born in South Carolina in 1928 and studied with the Katherine Dunham dance troupe in Paris. She appeared on Broadway in 1952's *New Faces*. Her early signature songs were "C'est si bon" and "An Old-Fashioned Girl."

Eartha Kitt has always been an earthy actress and singer, outspoken and courageous in expressing her views. She outraged the Johnson White House when she publicly questioned his administration's conduct of the Vietnam War during a luncheon in 1967, at which the First Lady was present. Her career was very nearly ruined. Her autobiography, *I'm Still Here*, appeared in 1989. Miss Kitt returned to national acclaim in the 1990s, again dazzling audiences with her artistry and musical talent.

"Santa Baby"

Mister "Claus," I feel as tho I know ya
So you won't mind if I should get familya, will ya?

Santa Baby, just slip a sable under the tree—for me.
Been an awful good girl, Santa Baby,
So hurry down the chimney tonight.

Santa Baby, a fifty-four convertible, too, light blue.
I'll wait up for you, dear Santa Baby,
So hurry down the chimney tonight.

Think of all the fun I've missed.
Think of all the fellas that I haven't kissed.
Next year I could be just as good
If you check off my Christmas list.

Santa Baby, I want a yacht and really that's not a lot.
Been an angel all year, Santa Baby,
So hurry down the chimney tonight.

Santa Baby, one little thing I really do need;
The deed to a platinum mine, Santa honey,
So hurry down the chimney tonight.

Santa cutie, and fill my stocking with a duplex and cheques.
Sign your X on the line, Santa cutie,
And hurry down the chimney tonight.

Come and trim my Christmas tree
With some decorations bought at Tiffany.
I really do believe in you.
Let's see if you believe in me.

Santa Baby, forgot to mention one little thing, a ring!
I don't mean on the phone, Santa Baby,
So hurry down the chimney tonight.

"SANTA CLAUS IS COMIN' TO TOWN"

This jaunty, singable tune first appeared in 1934. Popular singer and radio personality Eddie Cantor unveiled the new song on his weekly radio show. At first Cantor had rejected it as being too much of a "kiddie song." But Fred Coots, a song-writer for Cantor's radio program, apparently would not take no for an answer. He appealed to Cantor's wife, Ida, who liked the song, to use her influence on her husband. The ploy worked and she prevailed.

Cantor was a big hit at the 1934 Macy's Thanksgiving Day Parade, where he sang this jovial ditty just as Santa himself reached Macy's store on Herald Square. Once again, fate had intervened to make a song a hit.

The words to "Santa Claus Is Comin' to Town" were written by Haven Gillespie, a Kentucky-born songwriter who started out as a printer and even worked for *The New York Times* before beginning a songwriting career. Coots, who wrote the music, was a Brooklyn-born Vaudeville performer and songster. He wrote for musicals and was a favorite of Sophie Tucker.

Thirty years later *Newsweek* magazine did a retrospective on the musical careers of Coots and Gillespie. "Santa Claus Is Comin' To Town" had sold more than seventy million records since its release during the depression. Bing Crosby and Perry Como both had big hits with this delightful song.

George Hall's 1934 recording reached twelfth place on the *Billboard* charts that year. Other versions that attained popularity were the Four Seasons' recording in 1962 and the Jackson Five rendition in 1970.

"Santa Claus Is Comin' to Town"

You better watch out
You better not cry
Better not pout
I'm telling you why
Santa Claus is comin' to town.

He's making a list
And checking it twice;
Gonna find out who's naughty and nice.
Santa Claus is comin' to town.

He sees you when you're sleeping.
He knows when you're awake.
He knows if you've been bad or good,
So be good for goodness sake!

Oh! You better watch out!
You better not cry
Better not pout
I'm telling you why
Santa Claus is comin' to town.

"UP ON THE HOUSETOP"

This is one of the earliest American Christmas songs dealing with Santa Claus. It was probably written in the 1860s, which is when the character of Santa began to emerge as an icon in popular American Christmas celebrations. The terms "good old Santa" and "dear Santa" compete with "good Saint Nick," revealing that the author is hedging his bets about which term will eventually become the more familiar one. This brief song celebrates Santa's arrival with his reindeer on a typical rooftop, with toys for the children's stockings. A girl and her wish for a doll are the only specific references.

Benjamin R. Hanby (1833–1862), about whom little is known, is credited with the authorship of this song. Gene Autry and Bill Boyd, who portrayed Hopalong Cassidy on television, both recorded versions of "Up on the Housetop."

"Up on the Housetop"

Up on the housetop reindeer pause,
Out jumps good old Santa Claus;
Down thru the chimney with lots of toys,
All for the little ones, Christmas joys.

Ho, ho, ho,
Who wouldn't go!
Ho, ho, ho,
Who wouldn't go!

Up on the housetop,
Click, click, click,
Down thru the chimney with good Saint Nick.

Next comes the stocking of little Will
Oh, just see what a glorious fill
Here is a hammer and lots of tacks
Also a ball and a whip that cracks.

First comes the stocking of little Nell;
Oh, dear Santa, fill it well;
Give her a dollie that laughs and cries,
One that will open and shut her eyes.

Ho, ho, ho.
Who wouldn't go!
Ho, ho, ho,
Who wouldn't go!
Up on the housetop,
Click, click, click,
Down thru the chimney with good Saint Nick.

Ho, ho, ho,
Who wouldn't go!
Ho, ho, ho,
Who wouldn't go!
Up on the housetop,
Click, click, click,
Down thru the chimney with good Saint Nick.

SONGS FROM FILM
AND BROADWAY

The cinema and the theater have long been American passions. And the romance and fantasy that they convey have long captivated Americans, indeed the entire world, for the past century. They are cultural icons of the twentieth century, central to American popular culture.

In this section we tell the stories of five of the most popular songs of Christmas. All of them were written exclusively for these new media of entertainment, and all have fascinating histories.

"HAVE YOURSELF A MERRY LITTLE CHRISTMAS"

Hugh Martin and Ralph Blane wrote "Have Yourself a Merry Little Christmas" for the 1944 hit *Meet Me in Saint Louis*. This popular film, given four stars by Leonard Maltin, was directed by Vincente Minnelli and featured outstanding performances by Judy Garland, Mary Astor, Leon Ames, June Lockhart, and Margaret O'Brien, who won a special Oscar for the best child actress of the year. The film was released just before the last Christmas of World War II.

This musical comedy was based on Sally Benson's reminiscences of her life in turn-of-the-century Saint Louis, culminating in the Saint Louis World's Fair of 1903. The stories originally appeared in *The New Yorker* magazine.

Martin and Blane wrote a number of well-received songs for the film, including "The Boy Next Door." But "Have Yourself a Merry Little Christmas" has endured as a Christmas song classic.

Judy Garland is undoubtedly responsible for the song's success. Not only was her interpretation appropriate and affecting, but her instincts for the song's popularity were on target. She insisted on some textual revisions that changed the tone from bittersweet to hopeful. The original verse, "It may be your last, next year we will be living in the past" was transformed into the much more optimistic, "Let your heart be light, from now on our troubles will be out of sight." The context of the song is the family's impending move to New York City, against the wishes of all but the husband, who sees it as a positive career move.

The drowsy, romantic style of Garland made it an instant hit. Writes her recent biographer, David Shipman: "The delicacy and drama she brings to 'Have Yourself a Merry Little Christmas' remains a marvel."

The song was requested by audiences wherever the superstar appeared, and she always sang it on her CBS television

Christmas program. It was also a personal favorite of President John F. Kennedy, a friend of Garland's. In 1963 he told Garland, "We have changed our dinner hour at the White House so we can watch the show. It is our favorite show. Everyone at Hyannis Port listens, too. It is everybody's favorite show." This message heartened Judy, since her program had been in a ratings slump and faced possible cancellation. She taped her Christmas special just before the president's death. She sang her signature song and Mel Torme rendered his "Christmas Song." This was her favorite show. JFK's death shattered her, and she waged an unsuccessful fight with CBS president James Aubrey to do a special patriotic tribute in honor of the slain president.

Garland was always a trooper when it came to Christmas. In 1942 she was a headliner on the Elgin Watch Company's *Christmas Day Canteen*, a two-hour radio program honoring America's fighting men and women. But she will be forever associated with this song.

The composer/lyricists Martin and Blane collaborated on a number of songs, beginning with their first score for the 1941 musical, *Best Foot Forward*, starring Gene Kelly and June Allison. Martin was the arranger and vocal director of Cole Porter and Rodgers and Hart. In Hollywood he wrote songs for the *Ziegfeld Follies*, *Make a Wish*, and *High Spirits*. He also wrote for TV shows and for London musicals. The Birmingham, Alabama, native was the vocal coach for Lena Horne, Judy Garland, Nanette Fabray, Rosalind Russell, and Ray Bolger.

"Have Yourself a Merry Little Christmas"

Have yourself a merry little Christmas.
Let your heart be light,
From now on our troubles
Will be out of sight.

Have yourself a merry little Christmas,
Make the Yuletide gay,
From now on our troubles
Will be miles away.

Here we are as in olden days,
Happy golden days of yore,
Faithful friends who are dear to us
Gather near to us once more.

Through the years we all will be together
If the Fates allow,
Hang a shining star
Upon the highest bough.

And have yourself
A merry little Christmas now.

"SILVER BELLS"

This popular postwar carol (actually it appeared during the Korean War) has several distinctions. First, it is one of the few Christmas songs written for the movies that has endured on its

own. Second, and perhaps more importantly, it's the first American Christmas song that celebrates the joys of city life and the flavor of Christmastime in the hustle and bustle of urban areas. Finally, this song gave city dwellers a song that directly spoke to their unique experiences. It took a long time for someone to think that maybe America's city folks might like a carol of their own. After all, city dwellers had outnumbered their rural and small-town fellow citizens for many decades, but it was not until 1951 that "Silver Bells" was written.

The authors were Ray Evans, who was born in Salamanca, New York, and Jay Livingston, a McDonald, Pennsylvania, native. Both born in 1915, they collaborated and won Academy Awards for "Buttons and Bows" in 1948 and "Mona Lisa" in 1950. The next year they came together for this inspired song, which had its debut in the holiday film *The Lemon Drop Kid.*

In the film "Silver Bells" was a duet sung by Bob Hope and Marilyn Maxwell. The movie was based on a story by Damon Runyon, whose raffish, bottom-drawer characters pleased the reading public for a number of decades. The story had been filmed in 1934 and starred William Frawley, who also appeared in the 1951 version. Lloyd Nolan joined Hope, Maxwell, and Frawley in this film, which was directed by Sidney Lanfield. Film critic Leonard Maltin gave it three stars. Essentially a comedy, *The Lemon Drop Kid* is the story of a racetrack tout who owes big money to gangsters and must pay or else.

Bob Hope is one of America's truly beloved performers. He is long associated with Christmas, because of his many trips abroad to entertain America's military personnel. His Christmas program on television was an eagerly awaited annual event for many years.

In five low-key and graceful stanzas, Evans and Livingston conveyed the air of excitement, good feeling, and anticipation that seemed to mark Christmas in the city. Even familiar scenes take on a new life, with "sidewalks dressed in holiday style," ordinary traffic lights in red and green blending in the season, and everywhere the sound of silver bells heralding the joys of the season. People seem friendly and cheerful, despite the pressures of their lives, and the children are waiting with hope and expectation for "Santa's big scene."

One wonders if "Silver Bells" would have attained its great popularity had its original title, "Tinkle Bells," been used. Evans and Livingston told this background story in an interview in *Remember* magazine, a short-lived bimonthly published in Ambler, Pennsylvania. While writing this song for the film, they noticed a small silver bell reclining on Evans's desk. It tinkled softly and they thought this amusing title would be catchy. But Evans's wife couldn't stop laughing at that title, so they changed it to "Silver Bells," once again showing how important it is for songwriters and composers to listen to their spouses' opinions!

"Silver Bells" was a popular hit throughout the nation in the early 1950s, notably in versions by Bing Crosby and Al Martino. Radio Station WJAX in Jacksonville, Florida, sponsored an annual poll where listeners called in and voted for their favorite Christmas song. "Silver Bells" was the winner for several years.

Earl Grant's 1966 recording was immensely popular. Craig Pattillo's study of the *Billboard* popularity of more than two hundred Christmas songs from 1940 to 1982 found that Grant's version of "Silver Bells" was the ninth most popular.

This sentimental ballad was President John F. Kennedy's favorite Christmas song. His special assistant Dave Powers once asked a strolling band at a White House Christmas party to play "Silver Bells" at the president's request.

Neither Evans nor Livingston thought their little song would become immortal. But it has, and sales of all recorded versions have reportedly topped the 150-million mark.

"Silver Bells"

City sidewalks, busy sidewalks
Dressed in holiday style.

In the air there's a feeling of Christmas.
Children laughing, people passing
Meeting smile after smile,
And on every street corner you'll hear

Silver bells, silver bells
It's Christmas time in the city.
Ring-a-ling, hear them sing,
Soon it will be Christmas day.

Strings of street lights, even stop lights
Blink a bright red and green
As the shoppers rush
Home with their treasures.

Hear the snow crunch,
See the kids bunch.
This is Santa's big scene.
And above all this bustle you'll hear

Silver bells, silver bells
It's Christmas time in the city.
Ring-a-ling, hear them sing,
Soon it will be Christmas day.

"TOYLAND"

This is a kind of gentle, dreamy song written when the twentieth century was ripe and fresh, in 1903 to be exact. The song comes from *Babes in Toyland*, an operetta written that year by

Victor Herbert, the popular master of this musical genre, which is a kind of forerunner of the Broadway musical.

Herbert was born on the first of February, 1859, in Dublin, Ireland, home over the centuries to countless writers, artists, and musicians. He joined the trek of many of his countrymen to America and became a citizen in 1916. His music was on everyone's lips, it seems, as the nineteenth century gave way to the twentieth.

Herbert became the first American composer to write an original score for the new art form of the cinema, doing so for D. H. Griffith's brilliant but controversial *Birth of a Nation*. He also scored *Eileen*, a 1917 operetta set on the west coast of Ireland, and a 1922 Roaring Twenties extravaganza, *Orange Blossoms*.

His *Babes in Toyland* is based on characters from children's stories and fairy tales who come to life. There is a brief "Christmas fiesta" in the original. The plot line is simple: Little Jane and Alan flee from their miserly uncle and find refuge in a land of toys and childhood characters.

The short but sweet "Toyland" brings back happy memories of childhood even if it lacks a direct reference to Christmas.

Victor Herbert was a hero to Irish Americans. Among his songs are "God Spare the Emerald Isle" and "Old Ireland Shall Be Free." His 1924 funeral at New York's Saint Thomas Episcopal Church attracted throngs of admirers and mourners. A 1939 film biography, *The Great Victor Herbert*, starred Walter Connolly and Mary Martin. Films were adapted from his shows *Naughty Marietta* (which made stars of Nelson Eddy and Jeanette MacDonald) and *Sweethearts*.

The city of New York erected a statue of Herbert in Central Park in 1939. An even greater honor was accorded to his memory on May 13, 1940, when the United States government issued a postage stamp bearing his likeness.

Two film versions of *Babes in Toyland* were made. One in 1934 featured the comedic geniuses, Stan Laurel and Oliver Hardy. Critics then and now have loved this version. Contemporary film critic Leonard Maltin says it "looks better all the time." Oliver Hardy's biographer, John McCabe, called it "a delightful film that has won respectful critical notice through the years." It is now available in video under the title *March of the Wooden Soldiers*.

A 1961 Disney remake is universally regarded as inferior to the original, despite appearances by Ray Bolger, Tommy Sands, Annette Funicello, and Ed Wynn. Although the film has classic songs and visual gimmicks, Leonard Maltin says it is "colorful but contrived and has no substance or heart." A 1986 made-for-TV movie, starring Drew Barrymore, is even worse and is quite forgettable.

"Toyland" remains one of those odd little songs that has been adopted by the young in heart.

"Toyland"

When you've grown up, my dears
And are as old as I
You'll often ponder on the years

That roll so swiftly by, my dears,
That roll so swiftly by.
And of the many lands
You will have journeyed through.
You'll oft recall
The best of all,
The land your childhood knew!

When you've grown up, my dears
There comes a dreary day
When 'mid the locks of black appears
The first pale gleam of gray, my dears,
The first pale gleam of gray.
Then of the past you'll dream
As gray-haired grownups do.
And seek once more its phantom shore,
The land your childhood knew!

Toyland! Toyland!
Little girl and boy land,
While you dwell within it.
You are ever happy then.

Childhood's joy land,
Mystic merry toyland,
Once you pass its borders
You can ne'er return again.

"WE NEED A LITTLE CHRISTMAS"

This song is the only selection from a Broadway musical that has become a relatively popular Christmas song. It was written for *Mame*, a highly successful production that played for 1,508 consecutive performances on the Great White Way. Originally it was a quartet sung by the irrepressible Angela Lansbury and her colleagues Frankie Michaels, Jane Connell, and Sab Shimono.

The composer and lyricist for *Mame* was New York City native Jerry Herman. Herman studied drama at the University of Miami, then became a pianist in nightclubs before making it on Broadway. His early shows include *I Feel Wonderful* in 1954 and *Parade* in 1960. He won Tony awards for *Milk and Honey* (1961), *Hello Dolly* (1964), *Mame* (1966), and *La Cage Aux Folles* (1983).

Mame premiered at the Winter Garden Theatre in New York City on May 24, 1966. It was based on a play by Jerome Lawrence and Robert E. Lee and a novel by Patrick Dennis. A 1969 version was a hit in London and starred Ginger Rogers. The 1974 film version featured Lucille Ball as Mame. The show had a reprise on Broadway in 1983, again starring Angela Lansbury, and lasted 443 performances.

Mame is the tale of an unconventional woman named Mame Dennis, who has a penthouse apartment on Beekman Place on New York's famed Upper East Side. On December 1, 1928, "Auntie" Mame's ten-year-old nephew from Des Moines, Patrick, and his nanny, Agnes Gooch, arrive. The main action of the musical concerns the farcical misadventures of Mame's avant-garde crowd over a number of years.

"We Need a Little Christmas" occurs about midway through the play. A desperate mood has overtaken everyone, owing to the stock market crash and the financial disasters facing Mame. Though it is only a week after Thanksgiving, Mame proclaims the need for a little Christmas spirit "right this very minute" to bring back their lost happiness.

Mame admits that she has "grown a little leaner, colder, sadder, and older" and she desperately needs "a little angel sitting on my shoulder." So she tells everyone to "haul out the holly," "fill up the stocking," and "slice up the fruitcake." She pleads with Santa to "climb down the chimney" because "Santa, dear, we're in a hurry."

In his memoirs Jerry Herman said that this catchy tune literally "flew off the page" because his main character, Mame, "had to turn a disastrous situation into a joyous one." Herman added that Mame "made up her own rules." She believed, he wrote, that "you don't have to wait for a special day to celebrate Christmas. It was more important to celebrate Christmas when you need it."

Herman felt that this song almost wrote itself because it "brought out inner strengths in that woman that she didn't even know she had—that I didn't even know she had."

It all works well as a rousing tune that has survived on its own for three decades. Andy Williams, Julius La Rosa, and the New Christy Minstrels have recorded versions of it.

"We Need a Little Christmas"

Haul out the holly,
Put up the tree before my spirit falls again;
Fill up the stocking,
I may be rushing things but deck the halls again now.

For we need a little Christmas,
Right this very minute,
Candles in the window,
Carols at the spinet.
Yes, we need a little Christmas,
Right this very minute.
It hasn't snowed a single flurry,
But Santa, dear, we're in a hurry.

So climb down the chimney,
Turn on the brightest string of lights I've ever seen;
Slice up the fruitcake,
It's time we hung some tinsel on that evergreen bough.

For I've grown a little leaner,
Grown a little colder,
Grown a little sadder,
Grown a little older.
And I need a little angel,
Sitting on my shoulder,
Need a little Christmas now!

For we need a little music,
Need a little laughter,
Need a little singing
Ringing through the rafter,
And we need a little snappy "happy ever after,"
Need a little Christmas now!

"WHITE CHRISTMAS"

"White Christmas" is unquestionably America's most popular Christmas song. Its sales have never been surpassed—at least until Elton John's "Goodbye, England's Rose" ("Candle in the Wind, 1997"), a tribute to Diana, Princess of Wales, captured the imagination of the world in 1997. Still, "White Christmas" is the most popular Christmas single ever recorded.

Bing Crosby's recording alone sold more than thirty-one million copies, according to the *Guinness Book of World Records*. This remarkable achievement by the beloved songwriter Irving Berlin shows how the right timing, the right place, and the right lyrics often conspire to create a song that is so memorable and so appropriate to the occasion that its place in history is assured.

In 1940 Irving Berlin was a well-known, fifty-two-year-old composer of Broadway and show tunes, a radio personality (since 1928), and a lyricist for Hollywood. His "Easter Parade" was as much a part of Easter celebrations as egg hunts, and his moving "God Bless America" had become a second national anthem, able to move audiences as few songs ever had.

In 1940 Paramount Pictures induced Berlin to return to

Hollywood to score a new Bing Crosby-Fred Astaire film tentatively entitled *Holiday Inn*. It was to be a lighthearted musical about a singer's adventures refurbishing a country inn in Connecticut. A love story that continued and developed through a number of holidays, the film was designed to be a golden opportunity for a songwriter's creativity to blossom. And blossom it did. Originally, the cast thought Berlin's Valentine's Day song, "Be Careful, It's My Heart," would become the film's hit. But Berlin had other ideas. He saw the Christmas scene as climactic and wanted to celebrate it with lyrics that would be unforgettable. His musical director Walter Scharf was initially not impressed, telling Berlin biographer Michael Freedland that the song "seemed nice enough but no one thought it would be much else."

Berlin devoted all of his time and energy to fine-tuning what is undoubtedly his masterpiece. Sitting at a piano in Scharf's room at Paramount, he was oblivious to his surroundings until he had it just right. Even when Scharf told him not to stick around for Bing Crosby's taping, Berlin quietly did so anyway.

Berlin had a hands-on approach to his career. His contract for *Holiday Inn* stipulated that not a note of his music would be changed once filming commenced. And to make sure that things went right, he sat in on all story conferences and advised Crosby and Astaire on song interpretations and the intricacies of choreography. Bing Crosby remembered, "He lay down all sorts of laws. But he was very enthusiastic and somehow everyone else caught that enthusiasm. He'd make you share it. He wrote what was right for his singers. I'm lucky to have had him."

As the final scenes were completed, Crosby relaxed on the set and puffed on his pipe. He told Berlin, "I don't think you need to worry about this one, Irving."

The film was released in August 1942 but was not an enormous hit. Still, it built up an audience over the years and is now regarded as a classic Yuletide film. The song, of course, was immediately appreciated. It won the Oscar for best cinema song of 1942. Crosby introduced the single on his radio show, and his recording of it began to take off, though it was some years before it became the best seller of all times.

"White Christmas" is so nostalgic that it has a dreamlike quality, taking listeners back to the best Christmases of their lives. Even those who had never seen snow or whose Christmases were not generally white, could not help but admire its warmth and sentimentality. It was, in fact, American soldiers overseas who besieged Armed Forces Radio Services with requests to play the song that fueled its popularity. They made it the most requested song of the war years.

Berlin himself reflected on this turn of events. "It came out at a time when we were at war and it became a peace song in wartime, nothing I'd ever intended. It was nostalgic for a lot of boys who weren't home for Christmas. It just shows that inspiration can produce anything."

The song received another boost in 1954 when Hollywood decided to remake *Holiday Inn*. The new name? *White Christmas*, of course. This time the film was in color and the setting was changed to Vermont. But the story line was roughly the same, and Bing Crosby was featured once again. Fred Astaire was ill and had to be replaced by the ever-popular

Danny Kaye. Rosemary Clooney and Vera Ellen had major roles. The 1954 version proved popular, and Berlin's royalties for the title song reached a million dollars in 1955 alone. Berlin composed some new songs for *White Christmas*. "Count Your Blessings" became an immediate hit and has remained a standard inspirational song in many singers' repertories.

It is, perhaps, a tribute to the ecumenical spirit of America that a Russian Jewish immigrant with the birth name of Israel Baline should have written America's most cherished Christmas song. But one of his biographers, Laurence Bergreen, helps explain this unexpected development, writing that Berlin "had nostalgic memories of childhood Christmases on the Lower East Side, and especially of the Christmas tree belonging to his neighbors, the O'Haras. He, too, shared in its charms and warmth." Bergreen also wrote that Berlin consciously strove to make "White Christmas" simple, universal, and unforgettable. "With a subject as potent and evocative as Christmas, a few well-chosen words and images spoke volumes. His show business instincts were in complete command; he never paused to ponder the irony of a cantor's son writing an anthem about a day celebrating the birth of Jesus."

Berlin's phenomenal success with "White Christmas" also proves the importance of persistence. In 1909 he had written a Tin Pan Alley tune for the holiday called "Christmas Time Seems Years and Years Away." It was a flop. Can anyone remember it? Or even find a copy today? It is unlikely.

A touching anecdote shows how durable "White Christmas" is and how much it has become embedded in our hearts. A friend and neighbor of Berlin's, composer and singer John Wallowitch, used to gather some friends to sing "White Christmas" in front of Berlin's townhouse on Manhattan's East Side each Christmas Eve. Like the Waits of Victorian England, these wandering, amateur singers would serenade the composer. In 1983, when Berlin was ninety-five, they enjoyed a heartwarming experience. Laurence Bergreen tells the story:

> Christmas Eve 1983 was particularly cold—four degrees, with a nasty wind whipping off the East River. A friend suggested that they should try ringing Berlin's doorbell. "I found myself overcome with fear," Wallowitch said. "After what seemed an eternity I pushed the doorbell, and the house, which is usually dark, suddenly lit up like a Christmas tree. On the third floor, a shade was being pulled. We sang 'Always,' repeated 'White Christmas,' and then the front door opened."
>
> "Mr. Berlin wants to thank you," said a maid.
>
> "We're here to thank him," Wallowitch replied.
>
> The maid invited the freezing serenaders into the kitchen, where they were astonished to see Berlin himself, wearing pajamas, bathrobe, and slippers, his dark eyes large and bright. "I want to thank you," he told the group. "That's the nicest Christmas present I've ever had." The songwriter hugged all the men; it was, they noted, a good, strong hug, and then he kissed all the women.
>
> Afterward, the ecstatic little band returned to Wallowitch's apartment, where they sang songs by

Irving Berlin for two and a half hours without once repeating themselves. It had been, for them, a mystical experience; it was also the last time the songwriter ever appeared before an audience. (He died six years later at the ripe old age of 101.)

Irving Berlin was not a particularly modest man. Like Oscar Wilde, he was conscious of his own genius. He told a critic that the song was "my best since Easter Parade." To his staff he was more emphatic. "Not only is it the best song I ever wrote, it's the best song anybody ever wrote." Millions of listeners have echoed this observation for more than fifty years.

Bing Crosby's "White Christmas" was the number-one song of all songs charted by Billboard in 1942 and was the number one Christmas song in 1944, 1946, and 1947. Indeed, "White Christmas" was on the charts every year from 1942 to 1962. The song's staying power was reiterated in 1969 when the Crosby version was again the number-one Christmas song.

Bing Crosby was long identified with "White Christmas." His second wife, Kathryn, also had fond memories of this wonderful song. In the 1976 Christmas issue of *The Saturday Evening Post*, she remembered, "White Christmas is not a time of year, but a way of life for me. I met Bing during the filming of *White Christmas*. I'd heard the song over the years and loved it because it was a standard in our very flat state of Texas that had no snow at all."

Kathryn was, she says, "a blooming starlet on the Paramount Pictures lot" who had auditioned for a role in the film but was told she was "too sexy." When she met Bing, love soon blossomed. She told her readers, "From then on 'White Christmas' had an extra special ring to it. Every year when the movie plays on television and when Bing sings the song on our Christmas special, I think of the first time I heard it. It has become to me a melange of blue eyes, thoughtfulness, gentleness, courtesy, ease and consideration, capped by a great sense of fun that, to me, is Bing."

"White Christmas" is undoubtedly the most-recorded Christmas song of all time. It has been translated into dozens of languages including Dutch, Portuguese, Italian, French, and Spanish.

"White Christmas"

I'm dreaming of a white Christmas
Just like the ones I used to know,
Where the treetops glisten
And children listen
To hear sleigh bells in the snow.
I'm dreaming of a white Christmas
With ev'ry Christmas card I write:
"May your days be merry and bright,
And may all your Christmases be white."

VII

SPIRITUALS

The "Negro Spirituals" are a uniquely American contribution to musical history, arising as they did on the plantations of the Old South among African-American slaves. It is music from the heart, born of the experience of suffering. Arising spontaneously in a circumscribed culture, these songs often admit to no authorship. As in other folk cultures, they are part of oral tradition. They belonged to the community in which they arose, and now they belong to the world.

Gwendolin Sims Warren, in her wonderful book, *Ev'ry Time I Feel the Spirit*, tells about this heritage:

> Negro spirituals are true folk songs of the American experience, yet in a unique way. Most folk songs of other cultures and societies have been primarily secular, whereas the spirituals are sacred and religious. These spirituals cannot be attributed to individual authors, but to the musical and spiritual genius of the African-American people. Drawn from the Bible,

hymns, African styles of singing, and their creators' aspirations, experiences, and circumstances, the spirituals spoke of this world and of the next. They addressed a passionate longing for freedom and justice, and also embraced the virtues of Christianity: patience, love, freedom, faith, and hope.

Somewhat surprising, perhaps, is the dearth of Christmas songs in the spiritual tradition. There are a few, however, including "Go Tell It on the Mountain," and "Mary Had a Baby," which we discuss in this section. Some lesser-known ones are "Little Baby, Born in the Manger" and "Glory, Hallelujah, to the Newborn King."

Warren, drawing upon the work of James Weldon and J. Rosamund Johnson, who published two volumes of spirituals in 1926 and 1927, offers some explanations. One is that "African-Americans preferred to think of Jesus as God, as almighty, all powerful, rather than as an infant."

Another reason may be that in the early South "the anniversary of the birth of Jesus was not a sacred or religious holiday." This was probably not true, however, in Virginia, the Carolinas, and Florida, where Christmas was clearly celebrated in church and society (at least in some churches and by the government after the 1830s). William Gillmore Simms, the preeminent novelist of the Old South, depicts Christmas as a major holiday in the decades preceding the War Between the States, especially in his romance, *The Golden Christmas*.

For whatever reason, there is a relative scarcity of Christmas songs among the spirituals. Warren cites the Johnsons in their belief that "the majority of the nativity spirituals in existence belong to a period some time after Emancipation, when a new idea of Christmas and of Christ developed."

This is also reflected among white churches, which used Christmas hymns of European origin almost exclusively, since very few American composers or songwriters drew upon the ancient Christmas traditions until late in the nineteenth century.

Another view is expressed by musicologist and folklorist John W. Work. He wrote in 1961: "The Christmas spiritual is a folk song pearl. It is precious and very rare. Not one Christmas song is included in the well-known early collections of Negro Folk Songs. Not one Christmas expression has been uncovered in the five volumes of spirituals issued by Fisk University between 1873 and 1892."

Work suggests that "the explanation for the absence lies most likely in the worship calendar of the Negro folk church. This calendar provided no special service or any special place in the regular service for the Christmas celebration comparable to the Lord's Supper celebration once each month, which inspired the creation of the moving crucifixion songs."

Work's research in the area of religious folk music convinced him that Christmas spirituals developed outside of the church. He wrote: "Some of the Christmas spirituals were created by individual folk out of their personal joy and contemplation of the nativity event as a soliloquy or a colloquy with friends."

The origin is not as important as the fact that they exist and add joy and beauty to the musical repertoire.

Work adds, "The plaintiveness of the melodies, the quaint charm of the poetry, and the uniqueness of the Negro worshiper's concept of the nativity have made these songs singular additions to the carol concert program."*

"AS JOSEPH WAS A-WALKING"

This Appalachian spiritual might have its origin in the British Isles but it has clearly become identified with southern Appalachia. Several versions apparently exist.

This is one of the few carols that present Joseph's point of view, basing its story somewhat on Matthew's account of Joseph's encounter with the divine. The contrast between worldly wealth and the humble birth of Jesus is accomplished with rich imagery: a wooden cradle rather than silver or gold; spring water rather than wine; and a birth in an oxen's stall, not in a king's palace. The sixth stanza places the birth of Jesus on January 6, which suggests that this was written during the time of "old Christmas," before the changeover in the calendar, when Christmas was celebrated in the Southern Highlands on that day. Even today, in a few remote areas of Kentucky and North Carolina, Old Christmas is celebrated on January 6 (while others celebrate Epiphany).

This reference to "Old Christmas" clearly dates this folk carol to the seventeenth or early eighteenth centuries. Some of the language has elements of Old Elizabethan as modified in

*See John W. Work, "The Christmas Spiritual" in *Christmas 31* (1961), edited by Randolph E. Haugan and published by Augsburg Publishing House, Minneapolis.

the Southern Highlands: "a-walking" and "the elements shall tremble with glee." The last refrain "And Mary's Son at midnight was born to be our King" has nobility and character.

"As Joseph Was A-Walking"

As Joseph was a-walking, he heard an angel sing:
"This night shall be the birthnight of Christ, the heav'nly King;
This night shall be the birthnight of Christ, the heav'nly King."

"He neither shall be borned in house nor in the hall,
Nor in a king's palace, but in an oxen's stall;
Nor in a king's palace, but in an oxen's stall."

"He neither shall be washen in white wine nor in red,
But in the clear spring water with which we were christened.
But in the clear spring water with which we were christened."

"He neither shall be clothed in purple nor in pall,
But in the fair white linen that usen babies all.
But in the fair white linen that usen babies all."

"He neither shall be rocked in silver nor in gold,
But in a wooden cradle that rocks upon the mold.
But in a wooden cradle that rocks upon the mold."

"On the sixth day of January His birthday shall be,
When the stars and the elements shall tremble with glee.
When the stars and the elements shall tremble with glee."

As Joseph was a-walking, thus did the angel sing;
And Mary's Son at midnight was born to be our King.
And Mary's Son at midnight was born to be our King.

"GO TELL IT ON THE MOUNTAIN"

This rousing spiritual is a crowd pleaser. It adds life to any musical program. Originating most likely in the early 1800s, this song focuses on the shepherds and their reaction to the extraordinary birth.

This song was made popular by the Fisk University Jubilee Singers from Nashville, who toured the United States and Europe to raise scholarship funds for the college. This highly trained choral group has dazzled audiences for more than a century. They were beloved by Queen Victoria. In 1882 their appearance at the White House brought tears to the eyes of President Chester Arthur, a normally reserved man whose feelings were rarely expressed in public.

While its origins are unknown, there are some musicologists who believe its music could have been composed by Frederick Jerome Work, a Nashville-born composer and teacher, who died in 1942. His nephew, John Wesley Work, made this claim. Both men collected, preserved, and arranged many spirituals, including this popular one. John clearly adapted and arranged "Go Tell It on the Mountain" and helped make it a standard of the season.

"Go Tell It on the Mountain"

While shepherds kept their watching
O'er silent flocks by night,
When lo! throughout the heavens
There shone a holy light.

(Refrain:)
Oh!
Go tell it on the mountain,
Over the hills and ev'rywhere,
Go tell it on the mountain
That Jesus Christ is born!

The shepherds feared and trembled
When high above the earth
Rang out an angel chorus
To hail our Savior's birth.

(Refrain)

And lo! When they had heard it
They all bowed down to pray
And traveled on together
To where the Baby lay.

(Refrain)

When I was a seeker,
I sought both night and day,

I sought the Lord to help me,
And He showed me the way.

(Refrain)

He made me a watchman
Upon the city wall,
And if I am a Christian,
I am the least of all.

(Refrain)

Note: The words vary somewhat in different versions of this song.

"I WONDER AS I WANDER"

This hauntingly beautiful carol is an example of religious folk music that has been called "white spirituals," emanating as it does from the folk traditions and religious culture of Appalachia.

The four exceptional stanzas speak to the drama of Christ's birth from the point of view of an anonymous person pondering the meaning of the Nativity while "wandering out under the sky."

The language is authentic, simple, direct, and, unlike most cheery Christmas songs, this one links the birth of Jesus to his death, calling Him "the savior who did come for to die."

The words reflect the rural culture in which "I Wonder as I Wander" arose, mentioning that Mary "birthed" Jesus and adding "farmers," who are not mentioned in either Matthew or

Luke, as joining the wise men and shepherds. A nice Scottish touch can be seen in the use of "wee" in the third stanza, reflecting the Scotch-Irish heritage of much of Appalachia. Jesus, it is said, came to die "for poor on'ry people," an interesting way of defining humanity in its natural state! (The term could mean "ornery" or "ordinary.")

John Jacob Niles was a folksinger, folk music collector, and composer born in Louisville, Kentucky, in 1892. He began to collect and transcribe Appalachian folk music when he was fifteen and published several books of his researches and travels, including *Ten Christmas Carols* in 1935 and *Ballads and Tragic Legends* in 1937.

Niles was intrigued by this music when he heard a young girl sing it in a small North Carolina town. He asked her to repeat it, so he could transcribe it and preserve it for posterity. Its origins are not known with any certainty.

A teacher and an opera singer at one time, Niles wrote "Black Is the Color of My True Love's Hair" and "Jesus, Jesus, Rest Your Head," a charming and lyrical lullaby. A collection of his songs was published in 1975, five years before his death at Boot Hill Farm, near Lexington, Kentucky.

"I Wonder as I Wander"

I wonder as I wander out under the sky,
How Jesus the Savior did come for to die.

For poor on'ry people like you and like I;
I wonder as I wander out under the sky.

When Mary birthed Jesus, 'twas in a cow's stall,
With wise men and farmers and shepherds and all.
But high from God's heaven, a star's light did fall,
And the promise of ages it then did recall.

If Jesus had wanted for any wee thing,
A star in the sky or a bird on the wing,
Or all of God's angels in heav'n for to sing,
He surely could have it, 'cause He was the King.

I wonder as I wander out under the sky
How Jesus the Savior did come for to die.
For poor on'ry people like you and like I;
I wonder as I wander out under the sky.

"MARY HAD A BABY"

In common with a number of other spirituals, "Mary Had a Baby" highlights the maternal. Mary is seen as a mother with whom all can identify. Musicologist William Studwell observes: "Carols from black sources appear to have an especial fascination and affection for the fragile image of the blessed young woman and her helpless holy infant."

Several other African-American spirituals draw on the image of mother and child, including "Oh Mary, Where Is Your Baby?" and "Mary's Little Boy Child."

"Mary Had a Baby" probably originated in South Carolina during the days of slavery. It is clearly one of the most appealing spirituals, having as it does a theologically astute refrain, "The people keep-a-coming and the train done gone."

"Mary Had a Baby"

Mary had a baby, Oh Lord;
Mary had a baby, Oh my Lord;
Mary had a baby, Oh Lord;
The people keep a-coming and the train done gone.

What did she name Him? Oh Lord;
What did she name Him? Oh my Lord;
What did she name Him? Oh Lord;
The people keep a-coming and the train done gone.

She called Him Jesus, Oh Lord;
She called Him Jesus, Oh my Lord;
She called Him Jesus, Oh Lord;
The people keep a-coming and the train done gone.

Where was He born? Oh Lord;
Where was He Born? Oh My Lord;
Where was He Born? Oh Lord;
The people keep a-coming and the train done gone.

Born in a stable, Oh Lord;
Born in a stable, Oh my Lord;

Born in a stable, Oh Lord;
The people keep a-coming and the train done gone.

Where did they lay Him? Oh Lord;
Where did they lay Him? Oh my Lord;
Where did they lay Him? Oh Lord;
The people keep a-coming and the train done gone.

Laid Him in a manger, Oh Lord;
Laid Him in a manger, Oh my Lord;
Laid Him in a manger, Oh Lord;
The people keep a-coming and the train done gone.

"RISE UP, SHEPHERD, AND FOLLOW"

Published in 1867, this black spiritual likely dates from the end of the eighteenth century. It was one of the first spirituals to be published. Most of the others first saw publication in the twentieth century.

This gentle pastoral focuses on the shepherds, who are exhorted to leave their mundane activities "to follow the Star of Bethlehem." "Rise Up, Shepherd, and Follow" takes some poetic liberties with the biblical text, since it depicts the shepherds following the star of Bethlehem rather than the magi. ("The First Noel," of French origin, does the same!)

As the song is generally arranged today, a solo voice sings the verses, while a vocal ensemble intones "Rise up, shepherd, and follow."

Note: The words vary somewhat in different versions of this song.

"Rise Up, Shepherd, and Follow"

There's a star in the East on Christmas morn;
Rise up, shepherd, and follow!

It will lead to the place where the Savior's born;
Rise up, shepherd, and follow!

Leave your sheep and leave your lambs;
Rise up, shepherd, and follow!

Leave your ewes and leave your rams;
Rise up, shepherd, and follow!

Follow, follow!
Rise up, shepherd, and follow!

Follow the star of Bethlehem;
Rise up, shepherd, and follow!

VIII

WHIMSICAL SONGS

What would the Yuletide holiday be without some merriment and some hilarious misadventures? Many lovers of Christmas music are grateful to the songwriters who are able to see the funny side of this holiday season.

The lighthearted side of Christmas can be enjoyed in the four songs selected for this final section of our book. We decided to "leave 'em laughing."

May all of your Christmases be filled with joy and laughter.

"ALL I WANT FOR CHRISTMAS IS MY TWO FRONT TEETH"

This quirky song most likely could only have been written in the United States, where a spirit of gentle irreverence and put-downs of the solemn and pompous have a long history. "My Two Front Teeth" pokes mild fun at a common dilemma, the loss of front baby teeth by children. It is filled with the colloquial language of the 1940s, with repeated uses of words like "gosh" and "gee."

The song, written in 1946 by Donald Yetter Gardner, a Pennsylvania music teacher, was apparently the first of a series of humorous takeoffs on the otherwise solemn pageantry of Christmas. Obviously, songs like these appeal to some listeners more than to others. These whimsical ditties impart a kind of comic relief to the intensity of Christmas activities.

As one might expect, this unconventional song needed an unconventional popularizer, and a perfect match was achieved when Spike Jones decided to record it.

As is often true in the unpredictable music business, this song nearly didn't make it. Spike Jones's biographer Jordan R. Young describes what happened: "Don Gardner's 'All I Want for Christmas (Is My Two Front Teeth)' very nearly did not get recorded. The schoolteacher's composition—destined to become a holiday perennial—had been rejected all over town by the time it made its way to Jones. By then it was almost December—too late to get it out in time for Christmas. But he recorded it nonetheless."

Another reason for the song's eventual success was the role of George Rock, a vocalist and trumpet player known for his unusual vocal effects. Rock joined Spike Jones and the City Slickers immediately after the group's 1944 USO tour. His high-pitched childlike voice enhanced "All I Want," making listeners laugh all the way to the record stores.

Rock told Young that their choice of this unusual song was something of a fluke. The song apparently lay on a piano, and several of the troupe's members thought it was worth a try.

Rock experimented with sounds that might replicate missing front teeth until a certain whistling quality approximated the effect they all wanted. A songwriter with the Slickers, Eddie Brandt, apparently modified the music somewhat.

Young recounts: "When the record was finally issued a year later, the extra effort paid off; within six weeks, it reportedly sold 1.3 million copies. The record-buying public deluged Rock with some rather unusual fan mail—thousands of teeth, a pair at a time, in response to his plea." "All I Want" sold two million copies in its first year and became the number-one Christmas song of 1948.

Spike Jones was an authentic American original. He made

music that was funny, wacky, and outrageous. Dr. Demento, the syndicated radio personality, called Jones "a man whose name was synonymous with laughter in America for more than a decade," while Jordan Young wrote that he was "a man who defied convention and conformity."

Jones was born in Long Beach, California, in 1911. He took up the trombone and piano at age seven and received a set of drums for his eleventh birthday. After high school he played for dances, clubs, and radio stations with a Dixieland combo. He tried his hand at various gigs on the popular music scene, even becoming a studio musician for recordings, radio, and films.

In 1941 he established the City Slickers, who made their radio debut and soon signed a contract with RCA Victor for the Bluebird label. In 1942 they had their first hit, "Der Fuehrer's Face," a wild and wacky depiction of Adolph Hitler as a buffoon and a moron. It was a surprise hit as a Movietone News special and as a record.

Through the war years and after, Jones and the Slickers crisscrossed the country and appeared on CBS Radio. During the 1950s his parodies continued to please audiences, and he had his own television program on NBC in 1954 and on CBS in 1957. His show returned as a summer replacement on CBS in 1960 and 1961.

Jones recorded a few other offbeat Christmas songs such as "Barnyard Christmas," "Where Did My Snowman Go?" and "I Want Eddie Fisher for Christmas." All of them are happily forgotten. Jones collapsed at Harrah's Club in Lake Tahoe on March 23, 1965, and passed away at his Beverly Hills home on May 1 that year. He was fifty-three.

"All I Want for Christmas Is My Two Front Teeth"

Everybody stops and stares at me.
These two teeth are gone as you can see.
I don't know just who to blame for this catastrophe!
But my one wish on Christmas Eve
Is as plain as it can be!

All I want for Christmas is my two front teeth,
My two front teeth, see my two front teeth.
Gee, if I could only have my two front teeth,
Then I could wish you "Merry Christmas."

It seems so long since I could say,
"Sister Susie sitting on a thistle."
Gosh, oh gee, how happy I'd be
If I could only whistle.

All I want for Christmas is my two front teeth,
My two front teeth, see my two front teeth.
Gee, if I could only have my two front teeth,
Then I could wish you "Merry Christmas."

"THE CHIPMUNK SONG"

This Christmas novelty song was America's number-one Christmas song in 1958 and the tenth most popular since 1940. Its creator was Ross Bagdasarian, a Hollywood actor who had appeared in *Stalag 17* and in *Rear Window*, two popular films in the first part of the fifties. In 1950 he produced the Rosemary Clooney song, "Come On-a My House."

In September 1958 Bagdasarian, now using the pseudonym David Seville, got an idea that soon captivated the country. He said, "I recorded the song with half-speed little voices of my own and sang an introduction in my normal speech voice. When I finished the first recording, the voices sounded like butterflies, or mice, or rabbits, but most of all they sounded like chipmunks."

The song is about three chipmunks—Alvin, Simon, and Theodore—who can't wait until Christmas comes to bring them "toys and cheer." (The song is sometimes called "Christmas, Don't Be Late.") The charm is in the sound, not the words, and Seville won a Grammy for the best recording for children from the National Academy of Recording Arts and Sciences. He also won a Grammy for best comedy performance of the year.

The Chipmunks had a spin-off, of sorts. There was a television series in 1961–1962 based on the characters. A cartoon show also ran on television during the 1980s.

Bagdasarian/Seville died in 1972.

"The Chipmunk Song"

Christmas, Christmas time is near,
Time for toys and time for cheer.

We've been good, but we can't last
Hurry Christmas, hurry fast.

Want a plane that loops the loop.
Me, I want a hula hoop.
We can hardly stand the wait.
Please Christmas, don't be late.

"FROSTY THE SNOW MAN"

"Frosty the Snow Man," like "Rudolph the Red-Nosed Reindeer," is based on a children's story. Written in 1950 by Walter E. "Jack" Rollins, it soon found an audience of children who delighted in a tale of a playful snowman who had to move fast to avoid melting.

Most children, especially those native to cold winter climates, could identify with a snowman, and all children seem to love stories about inanimate objects who come to life and share experiences with them.

Frosty's creator, Rollins, and his music man, Steve Edward Nelson, had also created a new Easter character "Peter Cottontail" the year before. Their musical version of "Frosty" proved immensely popular in 1950 at Christmas even though the song does not even mention the holiday, unlike "Rudolph."

But the vision of a "jolly happy" snowman "with a corncob pipe, a button nose, a broomstick in his hand, two eyes made out of coal, and an old silk hat" caught on with listeners. Even Frosty's demise as the sun bore down on him was not too painful since he "waved good-bye," told his playmates not to cry, and promised them, "I'll be back again some day."

Gene Autry made this a Gold Certified single, selling more than a million records for Columbia. "Frosty" soon became a successful commercial venture and was packaged in several formats. In 1969 Jimmy Durante narrated a cartoon version of the tale on television, and Andy Griffith presented another rendering in 1979's *Frosty's Winter Wonderland*. Frosty and Rudolph had even gotten together in an earlier television show, in 1964, when the magical Frosty was seen as the host for a program celebrating Rudolph's adventures.

Other singers who had hits with Frosty include Ray Conniff, Vaughn Monroe, Roy Rogers, and Hank Snow.

"Frosty the Snow Man"

Frosty the snowman was a jolly happy soul
With a corncob pipe and a button nose
And two eyes made out of coal.
Frosty the snowman is a fairy tale they say.
He was made of snow but the children
Know how he came to life one day.
There must have been some magic in that
Old silk hat they found,
For when they placed it on his head,
He began to dance around.

Oh, Frosty the snowman
Was alive as he could be.
And the children say he could laugh

And play just the same as you and me.
Thumpety thump thump
Thumpety thump thump
Look at Frosty go.
Thumpety thump thump
Thumpety thump thump
Over the hills of snow.

Frosty the snowman knew
The sun was hot that day,
So he said, "Let's run
And we'll have some fun
Now before I melt away."
Down to the village
With a broomstick in his hand,
Running here and there
All around the square
Saying, "Catch me if you can."

He led them down the streets of town
Right to the traffic cop.
And he only paused a moment when
He heard him holler, "Stop!"
For Frosty the snowman
Had to hurry on his way,
But he waved good-bye saying,
"Don't you cry,
I'll be back again some day."
Thumpety thump thump

Thumpety thump thump
Look at Frosty go.
Thumpety thump thump
Thumpety thump thump
Over the hills of snow.

"I SAW MOMMY KISSING SANTA CLAUS"

Christmas 1952 saw this mildly amusing song rise to the top of the holiday charts, becoming the most popular Christmas song that year. Its success was undoubtedly due to Jimmy Boyd's rendition, which conveyed the bemusement and naiveté of a young child who catches Mom in a furtive kiss with the man in a snowy white beard. The little one is too young to realize that Santa is Daddy, or at least we think so, unless there was a little soap opera hanky-panky going on!

The charm lay in the presentation of the child's point of view by an unknown singer, Jimmy Boyd.

"I Saw Mommy" barely made it into this book because its words and music were written by an Englishman, Thomas P. "Tommie" Connor, who was born in London in 1904. The song received its greatest acceptance in America, however, and Jimmy Boyd was an American, so we included it.

Tommie Connor wrote the words and music to "Lilli Marlene," a popular World War II song. He also wrote the words for two other Christmas songs that never quite made it to the top. One was 1937's "The Little Boy That Santa Claus Forgot," with music by Michael Carr. The other was "I'm Sending a Letter to Santa," with music by Spencer Williams. In this song a little boy pleads with Santa for his soldier-father's safe return from the war. It brought tears to the eyes of British troops in France when Gracie Fields sang it to them.

Connor is still remembered for this little tune about a furtive kiss and a confused child's innocent response.

"I Saw Mommy Kissing Santa Claus"

Christmas toys all over the place,
Little Johnny wears a funny smile upon his face;
For Johnny has a secret,
And this secret he must share,
He wants to tell somebody,
So he tells his Teddy Bear:

I saw Mommy kissing Santa Claus,
Underneath the mistletoe last night;
She didn't see me creep
Down the stairs to have a peep,
She thought that I was tucked up
In my bedroom fast asleep.

Then I saw Mommy tickle Santa Claus,
Underneath his beard so snowy white.
Oh, what a laugh it would have been,
If Daddy had only seen
Mommy kissing Santa Claus last night.

SUGGESTIONS FOR FURTHER READING

Albright, Raymond W. *Focus on Infinity: A Life of Phillips Brooks*. New York: Macmillan, 1961.

Amburn, Ellis. *Dark Star: The Roy Orbison Story*. New York: Lyle Stuart, 1990.

Autry, Gene (with Mickey Herskowitz). *Back in the Saddle Again*. Garden City, New York: Doubleday, 1978.

Barnett, James H. *The American Christmas: A Study in National Culture*. New York: Macmillan, 1954.

Bergreen, Laurence. *As Thousands Cheer: The Life of Irving Berlin*. New York: Viking Penguin, 1990.

Binz, Stephen J. *Advent of the Savior; A Commentary on the Infancy Narratives of Jesus*. Collegeville, Minnesota: The Liturgical Press, 1996.

Cahn, Sammy. *I Should Care: The Sammy Cahn Story*. New York: Arbor House, 1974.

The Christmas Card Songbook. Milwaukee, Wisconsin: Hal Leonard Publishing Corporation, 1991.

Del Re, Gerard, and Patricia Del Re. *The Christmas Almanack*. New York: Doubleday, 1979.

Duncan, Edmondstoune. *The Story of the Carol*. New York: Scribners, 1911.

Emurian, Ernest K. *Stories of Christmas Carols*. Boston: W. A. Wilde Company, 1967.

Erlewine, Michael, ed. *All Music Guide*. San Francisco: Miller Freeman Books, 1994.

Ewen, David. *American Popular Songs*. New York: Random House, 1966.

Foley, Daniel. *Christmas in the Good Old Days*. Philadelphia: Chilton, 1961.

Freedland, Michael. *Irving Berlin*. New York: Stein and Day, 1974.

Gourse, Leslie. *Unforgettable: The Life and Mystique of Nat King Cole*. New York: St. Martin's Press, 1991.

Haskins, James (with Kathleen Benson). *Nat King Cole*. Briarcliff Manor, New York: Stein and Day, 1984.

Johnson, James Weldon, and J. Rosamund. *The Books of American Negro Spirituals*. New York: Da Capo Press, 1954.

Jones, Francis Arthur. *Famous Hymns and Their Authors*. London: Hodder and Stoughton, 1902.

Keyte, Hugh, and Andrew Parrott, eds. *The Shorter New Oxford Book of Carols*. New York: Oxford University Press, 1993.

Kirk, Elise K. *Music at the White House*. Urbana, Illinois: University of Illinois Press, 1986.

Marsh, Dave, and Steve Propes. *Merry Christmas, Baby: Holiday Music from Bing to Sting*. Boston: Little, Brown and Company, 1993.

Nettle, Reginald. *Christmas and Its Carols*. London: Faith Press, 1960.

Nissenbaum, Stephen. *The Battle for Christmas*. New York: Alfred A. Knopf, 1996.

Pattillo, Craig W. *Christmas on Record: Best Selling Xmas Singles and Albums of the Past 40 Years*. Portland, Oregon: Braemar Books, 1983.

Pelletier, Cathie, et al., eds. *A Country Music Christmas*. New York: Crown Publishers, 1996.

Restad, Penne L. *Christmas in America: A History*. New York: Oxford University Press, 1995.

Richards, Katharine L. *How Christmas Came to the Sunday Schools*. New York: Dodd, Mead, and Company, 1934.

Ryden, Ernest Edwin. *The Story of Christian Hymnody*. Philadelphia: Fortress Press, 1959.

Seeger, Ruth Crawford. *American Folk Songs for Christmas*. New York: Doubleday, 1953.

Shipman, David. *Judy Garland: The Secret Life of an American Legend*. New York: Hyperion, 1992.

Simon, Henry W., ed. *A Treasury of Christmas Songs and Carols*. Boston: Houghton Mifflin, 1973.

Smith, H. Augustine. *Lyric Religion: The Romance of Immortal Hymns*. New York: Fleming H. Revell Company, 1931.

Snyder, Philip. *December 25th*. New York: Dodd, Mead and Company, 1985.

Studwell, William. *The Christmas Carol Reader*. New York: The Haworth Press, Inc., 1995.

Sweet, Charles F. *A Champion of the Cross: The Life of John Henry Hopkins*. New York: James Pott and Co., 1894.

Torme, Mel. *It Wasn't All Velvet*. New York: Viking Penguin, 1988.

Warren, Gwendolin Sims. *Ev'ry Time I Feel the Spirit*. New York: Henry Holt, 1997.

Waters, Edward N. *Victor Herbert: A Life in Music*. New York: Macmillan, 1955.

Weiser, Francis X. *The Christmas Book*. New York: Harcourt, Brace and Company, 1952.

——. *Handbook of Christian Feasts and Customs*. New York: Harcourt, Brace and Company, 1958.

Wernecke, Herbert. *Christmas Songs and Their Stories*. Philadelphia: Westminster Press, 1957.

Young, Jordan R. *Spike Jones Off the Record: The Man Who Murdered Music*. Beverly Hills, California: Past Times Publishing Company, 1994.

ACKNOWLEDGMENTS

The authors gratefully acknowledge permission to reprint words to the following songs included in this book:

INDEX